# cape town
# WOT
# to do
# ☆ guide ☆

© All rights reserved. No part of this publication may be reproduced, stored in any retrieval system, or transmitted in any form or by any means, whether in part or whole, without express written permission by the publisher.

Places change, prices change, people change. In South Africa, a lot of things change. While every attempt is made to ensure that all information is correct at the time of going to press the publisher cannot accept responsibility for consequences arising from errors or omissions. Please notify of any mistakes or suggestions for future improvement. All feedback is greatly appreciated. We may even reward you with a prize for your efforts. Drop a line to Red Press, PO Box 23283, Claremont, 7735; or e-mail leger@mweb.co.za.

**Authors** Paul Leger & Carlos Amato
**Contributors** Brian Johnson-Barker & Jamie Cloete
**Editor** Paul Leger
**Illustration** Renée Krige
**Design & DTP** Caroline Cluver
**Publisher** Red Press
**Reproduction** CTP Book Printers
**Printer** CTP Book Printers

**A RED PRESS PUBLICATION
2001**

# a-z contents

## a
| | |
|---|---|
| abseiling | 3 |
| aerobatic flips | 3 |
| animal viewing | 4 |
| antique & junk shops | 6 |
| aquarium | 6 |
| architecture | 7 |
| art galleries | 9 |
| auctions | 12 |

## b
| | |
|---|---|
| ballooning | 13 |
| beaches | 14 |
| bead shops | 18 |
| birdwatching | 19 |
| boat cruises | 21 |
| Bo-Kaap | 23 |
| bookshops | 23 |
| braai spots | 24 |
| bungy jumping | 25 |

## c
| | |
|---|---|
| cableway | 26 |
| camel rides | 27 |
| Cape of Good Hope Nature Reserve | 27 |
| Castle of Good Hope | 28 |
| caving | 28 |
| classical music | 29 |
| classic car hire | 30 |
| comedy | 30 |
| Company Gardens | 31 |
| craft markets | 31 |
| cycling | 32 |

## d
| | |
|---|---|
| day trips | 34 |
| diving | 37 |
| drumming | 38 |

## f
| | |
|---|---|
| fly-fishing | 39 |

## g
| | |
|---|---|
| gambling | 40 |
| game fishing | 40 |
| gliding | 41 |
| go-karting | 41 |
| golf-driving ranges | 42 |
| Greenmarket Square | 43 |

### h
| | |
|---|---|
| helicopter flips | 43 |
| horseriding | 44 |
| Hout Bay | 45 |

### i
| | |
|---|---|
| ice-skating | 45 |

### j
| | |
|---|---|
| jetskiing | 46 |

### k
| | |
|---|---|
| kayaking | 46 |
| Kirstenbosch National Botanical Garden | 47 |
| kite-flying | 48 |
| kite-surfing | 48 |
| kloofing | 49 |

### l
| | |
|---|---|
| live music | 49 |

### m
| | |
|---|---|
| microlighting | 53 |
| motorbike & scooter hire | 53 |
| mountain biking | 54 |
| movies | 56 |
| museums | 57 |

### n
| | |
|---|---|
| nature reserves | 61 |
| nightlife: clubs & bars | 63 |

### p
| | |
|---|---|
| paragliding | 70 |
| penguins | 71 |
| picnics | 71 |
| planetariums | 73 |
| poetry readings | 73 |
| pool bars | 74 |
| putt-putt | 75 |

### q
| | |
|---|---|
| quad biking | 76 |

### r
| | |
|---|---|
| Ratanga Junction | 76 |
| record & CD shops | 77 |
| restaurants | 78 |
| Rhodes Memorial | 90 |
| Robben Island | 91 |
| rock-climbing | 92 |
| roller-blading | 92 |

**s**
- sandboarding — 93
- scenic drives — 93
- scratch patches — 94
- sex shops — 95
- shark diving — 95
- shopping malls — 96
- Signal Hill — 97
- skydiving — 97
- South African National Gallery — 98
- spectator sport — 99
- strip clubs — 100
- surfing — 100
- survival games — 102
- swimming pools — 102

**t**
- Table Mountain — 103
- ten-pin bowling — 104
- theatre — 105
- township tours — 107
- train trips — 108

**w**
- walks — 109
- Waterfront — 113
- whale-watching — 113
- windsurfing — 114
- wine routes — 115
- World of Birds — 121

**o**
- A-Z Index — 123

# •introduction

## saturday in the city

Riaan Cruywagen's toupee is fading, Freek's on another unspecial assignment. "Click!" JR's screwing Bobby, Sue Ellen's into relapse. "Click!" The Boks are a lost cause, the soccer's still a joke. "Click!" Hansie and Allan have made a million, Harksen is now at a trillion. "Click!"

Welcome to the Cape Town **Wot to Do Guide**, the guide that's guaranteed to get you off the couch and back into the world of the living – or, if nothing else, make you feel just a tad guilty staring at the ducks above the mantelpiece. As a with-it, on-the-ball Capetonian or visitor to the city, you've probably covered most bases and don't need this book, right?! Been there, done that, and have the T-shirt to prove it? The Waterfront, the Hout Bay ferry, the Cableway, the penguins, the bods at Clifton, sundowners at La Med, the slog up Lion's Head and the afternoon tea at Kirstenbosch, all comfortably tucked under your expanding belt, and nowhere else to go? Well then, read on...

Most will agree that our weird and wonderful mother of a city lying in the protective shadow of Table Mountain has heaps to offer. But few realize just how much. Setting out to compile this guide, the **Wot to Do** team certainly had no idea of everything that exists beyond the day to day humdrum of SABC1, N2 taxis and Telkom queues. Cape Town's list of leisure reads as a long single-ply roll of Chappies Did-You-Knows. For example: Did you know, you can go ten-pin bowling in Parow, ride a Camel on Noordhoek beach, do crazy barrel rolls 10 000 feet above planet earth, paraglide off Lion's Head, quaff beer in a shebeen, fine Cabernet under ancient oaks, spend quality time with a Great White shark, dangle from a rope off Table Mountain, press foot to floor in a world free of speed limits, watch your favourite local band beating out your favourite tune, leap out of a plane, explore the galaxy, hire a Harley, eyeball a crocodile, zeedonk, dinosaur and a funky sculpture, all in one day?

Over 100 weekend activities, all in and around Cape Town, all pretty easy to organise, and all (well, nearly all) affordable or free, the **Wot to Do Guide** will reveal just how much there is to do and see on this amazing toenail of Africa. It will also eliminate the slog of finding what you want to do when you want to do it. Virtually all the activities on the pages ahead demand nothing but a healthy appetite for life and in a few cases, a stomach for adventure. Very few demand previous experience or particular skill of any kind. Some will become a regular habit, others are better reserved for a special occasion, a midlife crisis or a sodden day. The choice is huge, with something for everyone and every mood.

The Cape Town **Wot to Do Guide** is about opening up to new opportunities, novel experiences and interesting Capetonians. It's about venturing where you haven't ventured before, letting your hair down, forgetting a frazzled week at work, feeding your body, mind and soul... But heck, most importantly, it's about having a damn good time. Enjoy!

**abseiling
aerobatic flips
animal viewing
antique & junk shops
aquarium
architecture
art galleries
auctions**

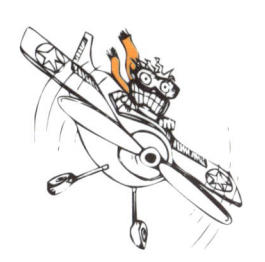

# • abseiling

Make like Spiderman – no formal training required, and no obligation to wear that kooky outfit. Abseiling is a fast-growing thrillseeker's racket that offers the intense drama of rock-climbing with an important modification – abseilers have gravity on their side. The idea is simple: a rope is fastened to a cliff-top and yourself, whereupon you dangle your way down, fending off the mountain with your legs and feeding rope through your harness. If you have the courage to open your eyes, the views are usually great and once you get the hang of it, the brief moments of flying are sweet. And where better to fly than among the mountains of the Western Cape? The three closest options are Table Mountain, Paarl Rock and the Steenbras River Gorge. A fair amount of guts is recommended but it's surprisingly safe and great fun – especially if you do it for no good reason.

### Abseil Africa
Operators of the world's highest commercial abseil – 112m down Table's Mountain's forehead. Also on the Abseil Africa cards is an outrageously dramatic abseil on Chapman's Peak: say a quick prayer to Aunt Bertha and hang out over the crashing waves of the Atlantic… For the slightly insane. Contact Adventure Village for the details and a 10% discount on any abseil trip on presentation of this book. 229B Long St, tel 424 1580, e-mail thrills@adventure-village.co.za, website www.adventure-village.co.za.

# • aerobatic flips

Out the way Tom Cruise, Top Gun II here we come. This is one way to view the world from a radically different perspective: fly upside down in a Pitts Special or Harvard Trainer. Both of which are not so much means of transport as mobile clothing. After donning your aeroplane, which you share with an experienced pilot with a perverse sense of humour, you're off into the wide blue yonder for an hour or so of gravity-defying, stomach-lurching thrill. Rolls, spins, dives, loops, and general showing off are the order of the day. Definitely not for the faint of heart or delicate of constitution. Booking is through the Harvard Club, tel 852 3038, cell 082-826 0885, e-mail jkb@netactive.co.za.

# animal viewing

Crocodiles, ostriches, butterflies, vultures, pelicans, hippos, snakes, zebra, wildebeest, chimps, penguins and bears, a few behind bars, others roaming free, Cape Town has representatives from most species – even zeedonk, a cross between a zebra and a donkey! While canned wildlife may not be your cup of tea odds of spotting a croc or grizzly in the Cape Town wild are more remote than meeting Winnie Mandela at an AWB braai, and fortunately, most of the city's zoos and animal sanctuaries offer the inmates a most comfortable life: free of predators and plenty of space to move about in. So whether your fetish is for leather, feathers or scales, chances are Cape Town will satisfy it.

### Butterfly World
Butterflies are the most glamorous members of the insect community, and you can schmooze with them at Butterfly World. It's a covered and temperature-controlled garden spanning 1000m$^2$ and home to 24 species of tropical butterfly from three continents. Their life cycles are staggered: you'll see larvae, pupae and fully-fledged butterflies throughout the year. Off R44, Klapmuts 9, tel 875 5628, e-mail esther@yebo.co.za, open daily 10am-4pm in winter, 9am-5pm in summer.

### Cape Point Ostrich Farm
Is it a bird, is it a dinosaur? Decide for yourself at the Cape Point Ostrich Farm, located about 400m from the entrance to the Cape of Good Hope Nature Reserve. Acquaint yourself with the day to day habits of this leggy bird and round off the experience with lunch or sundowners at the farm's tea garden. Tel 780 9294, e-mail cpof@iafrica.com, website www.capepointostrichfarm.com, open daily 9.30am-5.30pm.

### Clara Anna Fontein Game Reserve
Zebra, wildebeest and eland lead a laid-back existence at Clara Anna Fontein, a smart private game reserve at the foot of the Tygerberg hills which contains the last tract of indigenous renosterveld in the Western Cape. Luxury accommodation is provided in a restored Cape Dutch manor house, once owned by Elizabeth Verwey, the first independent woman farmer at the Cape. Vissershoek Rd, Durbanville, tel 975 1533, e-mail caflodge@iafrica.com, open 8am-5pm, visits by pre-arrangement only.

### Le Bonheur Crocodile Farm
Deep in the picturesque Paarl winelands there lives a thriving community of spine-chilling prehistoric reptiles. Le Bonheur Crocodile Farm is home to more than 2000 charming lizards, who can be seen tanning, swimming and eating copious amounts of sushi. There's a catch for these crocs, however – they're obliged to contribute to the manufacture of chic croc-leather shoes, bags and wallets, which are on display at the farm's Curio Shop. Not for the squeamish. Get there via the Babylonstoren Road outside Paarl. Tel 863 1142, e-mail lebonhr@mweb.co.za, open daily 9.30am-5pm.

## Monkey Town Primate Centre

Check out more than 20 different species of exotic monkeys from the Amazon. Among Monkey Town's 120 swinging tenants are spider monkeys, capuchins, marmosets and tamarins. You'll also find a licensed restaurant on the premises but keep a close eye on that banana split! Mondeor Rd (3km out of Somerset West towards Caledon), tel 856 2412, e-mail pro@monkeys.co.za website www.monkeys.co.za, open Mon-Sun 9am-6pm, entry R40 adults, R20 children.

## Rondevlei Nature Reserve

Over 200 bird species, including flamingoes and pelicans parade through Rondevlei's beautiful jigsaw of dense reeds and tranquil water. But the stars of this little-known wetland reserve are the local hippos – they don't do much by day, but there's plenty evidence of decadent nocturnal marauding. Telescopes and lookout towers are conveniently situated around the sanctuary. Access is from Victoria Rd into Fisherman's Walk Rd, Grassy Park. Tel 706 2404, e-mail rondevlei@sybaweb.co.za, open daily, 8am-5pm (longer in December), R5 entrance fee.

## The Snake Centre

Ever since Mr Serpent offered Eve an apple in the Garden of Eden, snakes have been treated as the bad guys of the animal kingdom. If you share this view and if these hapless creatures are the stuff of your nightmares a trip to the Snake Centre in Paarl may lead to a change of heart. On show at this breeding and conservation centre are 36 different species of slithery reptile, as well as tortoises, lizards, leguans and other prehistoric creatures. Access to the Snake Centre is via Main St in Paarl and then along the R45 towards Malmesbury. Tel 863 8309, open Mon-Sat 9am-5.30pm, closed Sundays.

## Spier Cheetah Park

With several restaurants, picnic spots and a platter of live entertainment close at hand, Spier Estate is a satisfying family outing; and for those with an interest in wildlife there is a family of resident cheetahs. Enjoy a close-up view of these zippy creatures, followed by a picnic on the manicured lawns – ingredients supplied by Spier's Farmstall deli. The cheetah park relies entirely on public support so the R35 entry fee is money well spent. Spier Estate, Stellenbosch, tel 809 1188, e-mail cheeta@intekom.co.za, website www.cheetah.co.za, open daily 10am-5pm.

## Tygerberg Zoo

Chimpanzees, lions, leopards, crocodiles and an arkload of other creatures can be seen at Tygerberg Zoo. Rare and threatened species are bred here, and the weird and wonderful tenants are well cared for, considering the shoestring budget. But, as in any zoo, the larger animals live in enclosures that seem a little too small for comfort. Klipheuwel/Stellenbosch exit off N1 towards Paarl, tel 884 4494, e-mail tzt@kingsley.co.za, open daily 9am-5pm.

## Wiesenhof

A menagerie of antelope, cheetahs, ostriches, wildebeest and baboons can be viewed at Wiesenhof. Apart from the animals, the park has a swimming pool, braai and picnic facilities, and a coffee shop. Get there by taking the R44 Klapmuts exit (off N1) and proceed for 4km. Tel 875 5181, open 9.30am-6pm (closed Mondays), entry R17 adults, R11 children.

**World of Birds**

If it's got a beak, there's a fair chance you'll cross paths with it at the World of Birds, one of the largest bird parks on the planet. More than 330 species have their lodgings here, from bite-sized white-eyes to psychedelic macaws to Mad Max vultures and mystical owls. The park consists of over 100 walk-through aviaries: mammalian visitors are utterly ignored, passing incognito through a magical, fantastically diverse feathered universe. A captivating experience. Valley Rd, Hout Bay, tel 790 2730, website www.worldofbirds.org.za, open daily 9am-5pm. (See also page 121)

# •antique & junk shops

Yep, those thatch-roofed, gabled homesteads do have attics. And yes, the contents are brought into town every now and then, and sold – some by public auction, others through antique and junk dealers. The prospect of a bargain is always present but there's usually a fairly long queue of eager buyers waiting to snap it up. But then again, the experience of searching for something is often as satisfying as the acquisition itself. In the city centre most stalls appear from Monday to Saturday in and around Church Street. There are heaps of antique-cum-junk shops in this area – Greenmarket Square often has good pieces tucked away among the bad and Long Street has a growing number of specialised and general dealers. Heading south, Groot Constantia and Muizenberg set up stalls at weekends and the Main Road through Kalk Bay is lined with shops ready to trap the unwitting with inflated prices. Where one finds antique shops one tends also to find coffee shops and restaurants – the result is usually a most agreeable combination of activities. So whether it's a Royal Family beer mug or a Victorian chamber-pot like gran used to own, chances are you'll find it somewhere, sometime.

# •the aquarium

A huge underwater nature reserve full of wonder and weirdness, the Two Oceans Aquarium at the V&A Waterfront will enthral you even if you have only a passing interest in fish. Among the residents are giant extra-terrestrial-like crabs, exquisite luminous jellies, ragged-tooth sharks and slithering eels of all shapes and sizes. The I&J Predator Exhibit is not to be missed, particularly when the sleek predators of the deep have their lunch on Sundays. Spending time at the Indian Ocean tropical exhibit is like stepping into an underwater dream: the tropical fish here flaunt outrageous lumo outfits that would put Gaultier to shame. At the touch pool, you can stroke anemones and fondle starfish. For qualified divers, a pool of a different kind awaits you – take the plunge and dive with the sharks. The aquarium is a tantalizing window into a breathtaking underwater universe. Have a look. Dock Road, V&A Waterfront, tel 418 3823, website www.aquarium.co.za, email aquarium@aquarium.co.za, open daily 9.30am-6pm, entrance fees adults: R40, children 4-17 years R20 (under 4's free), and students/pensioners R30. Prices subject to change without notice. Consider a Solemates membership for R65 (adults) and R35 (children) and visit as many times as you like for a year.

## •architecture

Living in and among beautiful buildings is good for one's general well-being – and Cape Town has enough architectural quality and interest to fill a string of healthy Sundays. The only way to appreciate this diversity is on foot – anything faster and you'll miss the varying architectural styles and the subtle decorative features. While the city centre boasts some of the most migraine-inducing slabs of concrete ever scraped from the modernist barrel – the Cape Town Civic Centre being but one example – there's a rich vernacular tradition spanning four centuries, and several free-spirited recent buildings.

The first permanent shelters to be built at the Cape were the spacious homesteads of the early Dutch settlers. The main features of these graceful homes have been recycled by Cape architects ever since: chunky limewashed walls, thatched roofs, vine-shaded stoeps and, most distinctively, curvilinear gables giving a sedate flourish to the long front wall.

The late 1800's brought a stiff dose of British design sensibility to the Cape and with it a crop of lofty imperial public buildings appeared. The city was mushrooming during this period and the Victorian aesthetic flourished in the thousands of new houses and shops in Woodstock, Observatory and Rondebosch.

The city's 20th century architectural legacy is not so nice. A handful of jazzy Art Deco office blocks were built in the prewar era, but thereafter the dominant aesthetic was a grim apartheid take on the International Style. The newly-reclaimed Foreshore became an Orwellian no-man's land – full of wind, textured concrete and bureaucrats. It was only in the 80's and 90's that a lighter touch appeared in buildings like Safmarine House – a pyramid-topped skyscraper – and shopping developments like the postmodern Victoria Wharf Centre, which features a transparent steel-and-glass roof and a whimsical, engaging facade.

### City Centre

A good introduction to Cape Town's architectural heritage is the Castle of Good Hope, a glowering fortress at the bottom of Buitenkant Street. The oldest surviving building in South Africa, the Castle was erected by the Dutch East India Company in 1665 on ground that was then at the water's edge. Nearby, on Darling Street, is the City Hall (1905), a calm and impressive Edwardian building whose clock is a precise replica of London's Big Ben. Close by is the Old Mutual building, a chunky example of South Africanised Art Deco. On Adderley Street you'll find the Standard Bank building (1880), a huge and solemn stone monument to the Victorian gods of commerce and empire, and the 18th-century Slave Lodge (Cultural History Museum), whose facade was designed by Louis Michel Thibault, one of the foremost Cape Dutch architects. At the bottom of Government Avenue are the Houses of Parliament (1884), an opulent neo-classical affair with undeniable gravity and balance. Within the Company Gardens are all the long-faced influences of Transvaal Town Hall (South African Museum), Cape Revival (Tuynhuys), Greek Revival (South African Library) and Edwardian Gothic (St George's Cathedral). On Greenmarket Square is the placidly understated Old Town House (1755), which combines the Cape Dutch idiom mixed with neo-classical flourishes. In rainy weather slaves used to gather and shoot the breeze under its portico, which hence became known as the "slave's portico". Also on the Square are two of the city's most exuberant examples of Art Deco: Market House and Namaqua House. Strolling up to Long Street you'll see rows of double-storey Victorian shops, whose filigreed balconies and delicate vertical lines make it one of Cape Town's feelgood streets.

### Bo-Kaap

The nucleus of Bo-Kaap is made up of narrow roadways lined by small Georgian cottages with plain facades and flat roofs that you'll only notice if you look down over the area from Signal Hill. Rose Street, Chiappini Street and Upper Longmarket Street all contain good examples of the style. Also to be found in the neighbourhood are a number of mosques – although representing different styles, all are unmistakably Oriental and each with a tower from which Muslims are called to prayer. First timers to Bo-Kaap are advised to join the official Bo-Kaap Guided Tour (tel 422 1554), an informative trip down yesteryear that includes a visit to a mosque.

### Wine Estates

Thatch and gables conjure up the popular image of the old Cape homestead, with examples to be seen close to the city and throughout the Winelands. Among the finer local examples are Groot Constantia, built in 1692, Buitenverwachting and Klein Constantia, all enhanced by beautiful settings and fine wine. Tokai Manor House (1795), although not open to the public is an interesting blend of Cape Dutch and elegant French Neoclassicism, while Kronendal in Hout Bay (1800), is another excellent example of a Cape Dutch homestead. Typical of the Cape Dutch style are elaborate gables (front and end), a thatched roof, small-paned windows and a façade that's usually symmetrical about the central front door. End gables provided some wind-resistance for the thatch, and created space for windows to illuminate the often extensive attic. Front gables, often elaborate – the more extravagant your gable the greater your status –

also let light into the attic and, in the event of fire, prevented a stream of burning thatch from cascading onto the heads of people fleeing through the front door. Dread of fire led to the replacement of this Cape Dutch style in Cape Town by houses similar to those of the Bo-Kaap (flat roofs and flush facades), but the style was promoted by the British architect Herbert Baker around the end of the 19th century, as Cape Dutch Revival.

### Woodstock & Observatory
Older suburbs such as Woodstock, Salt River and Observatory still have rows of model housing, suited to the aspirations of blue-collar Victorian workers. Further afield, employers sometimes built modest 'model estates' for their employees, as at old Irish Town in Newlands, where brewery workers were housed. Examples of Victorian architecture range from palatial mansions to semi-detached artisan's cottages. Many are truly beautiful buildings, with intricate pressed ceilings, stately wooden staircases, and wrought-iron "broekie-lace" verandas, so-called because they inspired thoughts of lacy underwear.

### Guided City Walk
If you can't tell Victorian from Georgian from Cape Dutch, for a mere R50 you can join local guide and writer Ursula Stevens on a guided walk through the historic city centre and Company Gardens. This interesting stroll through the past departs Monday to Friday at 11am from the Cape Town Tourism Centre, located on the corner of Berg and Castle St. Tel 426 4260.

# •art galleries

It has been suggested that you can see a city's soul through its art galleries, and on this sunny toe of Africa the maxim seems to hold true: like the city at large, Cape Town's art culture is perverse, divided, self-involved and often a bit insane. But don't let this put you off: there's a wide and exciting range of artistic output to be trawled through, including inexplicable postmodern installations, jazzy township-life linocuts, bawdy cartoon light-fittings and mystical landscape photography. Of late there's been an exciting movement towards event-based art, in which music, performance and viewer participation are integrated into the visual product. Check these out – events are promoted in the daily papers and the Mail and Guardian. If you're more interested in finding something natty to hang above your fireplace, the city's many traditional galleries harbour an abundance of paintings, prints and sculptures. Prices range between the cost of a retread and the cost of a used minibus.

### 3rd i Gallery
An airy loft on the city centre periphery, showcasing the talent of upcoming local artists and photographers. A framing service is also available.

95 Waterkant St, Cape Town, tel 425 2266, e-mail fcinciii@iafrica.com, open Mon-Thu 9am-6pm, Fri 9am-5pm, Sat 9.30am-1pm.

## Arts Association of Bellville & Bellville Art Centre
Bellville's artistic nerve-centre, this is a warm and unpretentious gallery with a selection of paintings, sculpture and artefacts. Music concerts are also held here, as well as a wide range of art and craft classes. Library Centre, Carel van Aswegen St, Bellville, tel 918 2301, e-mail artb@icon.co.za, open Mon-Fri 9am-8pm, Sat 9am-5pm.

## Association for Visual Arts
An intriguing and inspiring collection of contemporary artworks can be seen at the AVA, which exhibits and promotes a wide range of Capetonian artists on a non-profit basis. A range of media and strands of the city's art scene are featured. Metropolitan Gallery, 35 Church St, tel 424 7436, e-mail avaart@iafrica.com, website www.ava.co.za, open Mon-Fri 10am-5pm, Sat & Sun 10am-1pm.

## Bang the Gallery
An essential station on the gallery circuit, Bang the Gallery is a smallish but funky art space that carries exhibitions by dynamic young artists, sculptors and photographers. 21 Pepper St, Cape Town, tel 422 1477, e-mail alexh@bangthegallery.co.za, website www.bangthegallery.co.za, open Mon-Fri 10am-5pm, Sat 10am-2pm.

## Beezy Bailey Art Factory
One of Cape Town's most prolific and adventurous artists, Beezy Bailey's Art Factory incorporates a homeware store, a ceramic studio, a gallery and a coffee bar. The building's facade is decorated with outlandishly brilliant dream images – check it out. 4 Buiten St, tel 423 4195, e-mail beezy@beezybailey.co.za, website www.beezybailey.co.za, open Mon–Fri 9.30am–4.30pm, Sat 9am–1pm.

## Brendon Bell-Roberts Gallery
A young gallery committed to mounting bold and inventive group exhibitions. Young painters, sculptors and photographers take centre stage in a simple, elegant space. 199 Loop St, tel 422 1100, e-mail dps@icon.co.za, website www.bell-roberts.com, open Mon-Fri 8.30am-5pm, Sat 9am-1pm.

## The Cape Gallery
Crowded with atmospheric landscapes, nature studies and cityscapes, the Cape Gallery is a longstanding player on the local art circuit and a good stop-off if you're after quality figurative paintings. Common to most of the works is an intrinsically South African theme that reflects an abiding love of the land. The works are mainstream but there's a very useful range. 60 Church St, tel 423 5309, e-mail cgallery@mweb.co.za, website www.capegallery.co.za, open Mon-Fri 9.30am-5pm, Sat 9.30am-1pm.

## Everard Read Gallery
An upmarket gallery showcasing a range of high-end contemporary South African artists, aimed at the well-heeled and serious collector. 3 Portswood Rd, Block D, Portswood Close, V&A Waterfront, tel 418 4527/8, e-mail ctgallery@everard.co.za, open Mon-Sat 9am-6pm.

## Hänel Gallery
Based in both Cape Town and Frankfurt, Germany, the Hänel Gallery carries a strong line-up of international and South African artists, from Robert

Rauschenberg to Lisa Brice. Much of the work here is somewhat academic, with an emphasis on installations and conceptual pieces. 84 Shortmarket St, tel 423 1406, open Tues-Fri 11am-5pm, Sat 10am-4pm.

## Hout Bay Gallery
Contemporary artwork, sculpture and ceramics are on display, and among the artists represented at the Hout Bay Gallery are painter Paul du Toit and fine art photographer Harry de Zitter. A framing service and art supplies are also available. 112 Main Rd, Hout Bay, tel 790 3618, e-mail art@houtbaygallery.co.za, website www.houtbaygallery.co.za, open Mon-Fri 9am-6pm, Sat 10am-6pm, Sun 11am-4pm.

## Imhoff Farm
Imhoff is an 18th century farm shared by an art collective, restaurant, nature park, as well as (captive) snakes, camels and horses. Wander through the studios and see painters, potters, textile and stained-glass makers on the job in a relaxed atmosphere. Kommetjie Rd, Kommetjie, tel 783 4545, e-mail imhoff@naturefarm.co.za, open Tues-Sun.

## João Ferreira
The João Ferreira gallery has a dual focus: it promotes cutting-edge and wet-behind-the-ears artists in its downstairs showroom, while also dealing in the works of old luminaries such as Walter Battiss and well-known international artists. One of Cape Town's more progressive art-spaces. 80 Hout St, tel 423 5403, e-mail joao@iafrica.com, open Tues-Fri 10am-5pm, Sat 10am-2pm.

## Johans Borman Fine Art Gallery
A smart gallery with an impressive collection of paintings by canonic South African artists such as Irma Stern, Gregoire Boonzaier and Hans Pierneef. Contemporary figurative painters such as Erik Laubscher are also represented. Infin Art Building, 60 New Church St, tel 423 6075, e-mail joao@iafrica.com, open Mon-Fri 10am-6pm, Sat 9am-2pm.

## Kalk Bay Gallery
The fine art heartbeat of the rootsy harbour village, the Kalk Bay Gallery makes for excellent Sunday browsing terrain. It boasts a multifarious collection of original paintings, limited edition graphics, engravings, prints, African art and artefacts. 62 Main Rd, Kalk Bay, tel 788 1674, e-mail far@iafrica.com, open daily 9am-5pm.

## Marvol Museum of Russian Art & Culture
An outlandish outpost of ancient Slav civilisation in the heart of Kuils River, the Marvol Museum is home to a fine collection of Russian paintings, decorative art, Orthodox icons and Fabergé Easter eggs. Lectures and video screenings happen here, and coffee and snacks are for sale. Hazendal Wine Estate, Bottlery Rd (M23), Kuils River, tel 903 5112, e-mail hazen@icon.co.za, open Tues-Fri 10am-4pm, Sat-Sun 10am-3pm, guided tours 10.30am and 2.30pm.

## Montebello Design Centre
The Montebello Design Centre is home to a smattering of artists and craftspeople, from ceramicists to makers of African musical instruments to papermakers and painters. On the same site, under towering trees, you'll find the Gardeners Cottage, a pleasant eatery for breakfast, lunch or tea. 31 Newlands Ave, Newlands, tel 685 6445, open Mon-Fri 9am-5pm, Sat 9am-3pm, Sun 10am-3pm.

### Noordhoek Art Gallery
Part of the art, craft and farm-produce mecca that is the Noordhoek Farm Village. Here you can view quality ceramic art, painted fabrics, Berber jewellery and a varied range of paintings. The Village offers good food and the chance to see resident artists and craftspeople at work. Shop 10, Werkswinkel, Noordhoek Farm Village, tel 789 2287, e-mail info@degoede.co.za, open 9.30am-5.30pm daily.

### The Peanut Gallery
Promoting and showcasing the works of young emerging local artists is the mission of this gallery owned by artist Gerard Cloete. On display is a range of affordable art, much of it yet to filter into public consciousness. 66 Church St, Cape Town, tel 426 5404, cell 082-973 4189, open Mon-Fri 9am-4.30pm, Sat 9am-1pm.

### Rembrandt van Rijn Art Gallery
Visit the Rembrandt van Rijn in Stellenbosch to see some superb contemporary works by the likes of Penny Siopis and William Kentridge, as well as Anton van Wouw bronzes and Irma Stern paintings. Haughty but well-stocked. 31 Dorp St, Stellenbosch, tel 886 4340, e-mail deh@remgro.com, open Mon-Fri 9am-12.45pm, 2pm-5pm, Sat 10am-1pm, 2pm-5pm.

### Rose Korber Art Consultancy
An upmarket dealership and gallery showcasing an impressive array of contemporary South African, African and international art, beadwork, ceramics and tapestries. 48 Sedgemoor Rd, Camps Bay, tel 438 9152, open Mon-Fri 9am-5pm.

### South African National Gallery
A world-class gallery with an intriguing permanent collection of Southern African and international art. Among the works on view are Jane Alexander's chilling sculpture The Butcher Boys and a charmingly unprophetic 1897 painting titled Holiday Time in Cape Town in the Twentieth Century. The SANG also hosts a wide variety of inventive and inspiring exhibitions from around the world. Unmissable. Government Ave, Cape Town, tel 465 1628, e-mail sang@gem.co.za, website www.museum.org.za, open Tues-Sun 10am-5pm, entry R5.

### UCT Irma Stern Museum
Paintings and sculptures by Irma Stern, one of South Africa's greatest artists are exhibited in the house she lived in. Stern's superb collection of African and European artwork is also displayed here. An evocative, serene place, the Museum has a beautiful enclosed garden. Cecil Rd, Rosebank, tel 6855686 e-mailbpettit@protem.uct.ac.za, website www.museums.org.za/irma, open Tues-Sat 10am-5pm.

### University of Stellenbosch Art Gallery
A showcase for Stellenbosch's vigorous art scene, the gallery hosts regular exhibitions by young painters, sculptors and photographers. Well worth keeping tabs on. Cnr Bird & Dorp St, Stellenbosch, tel 808 3693, open Mon-Fri 9am-5pm, Sat 9am-1pm.

# •auctions

Cape Town auction sales can be great entertainment and excellent places for picking up new treasures and old junk.

The spice is in the range of goods rather than the prices. In fact, prices are not likely to be significantly lower than anywhere else in the country, but it's a popular belief – and one that's hard to shake – that Cape Town is some sort of magical fount of bargain-priced antiques. Maybe you'll prove it right. In the city centre Ashbey's Galleries on 43 Church Street (tel 423 8060), holds the most regular and interesting antique auction sale, with auctions every Thursday at 9.30am. On Langeberg Rd, Durbanville, jewellery and silver falls under Kenny Finberg's hammer (tel 988 7766), while to the south, Hofmeyr-Mills at 13 Piers Rd, Wynberg (tel 761 1803) buzzes every Thursday and Saturday at 9.30am, with everything from fondue sets to art deco couches up for grabs. Check the local newspapers, especially the Cape Times, Cape Argus and Die Burger, for upcoming auctions, including those in Stellenbosch, Paarl and other towns within easy range.

**ballooning**
**beaches**
**bead shops**
**birdwatching**
**boat cruises**
**bo-kaap**
**bookshops**
**braai spots**

## •ballooning

It may not be the most practical means of aviation ever invented – no steering wheel or rudder to speak of, and an oversized picnic basket for a cockpit – but the idea of floating silently above the earth in the wake of eagles, is incredibly alluring. While conditions for hot-air ballooning in this neck of the woods are not exactly ideal, what with the Cape Doctor doing his regular rounds, this hasn't stopped German couple Carmen and Udo of Winelands Ballooning from lighting the burner every summer and guiding flights of fancy over the vineyards. If you have R1000 or so to spare, you too can join them at sunrise between November and April, and play Richard Branson for an hour. Back on the ground, Carmen and Udo will treat you to a lavish champagne breakfast at the famous Grand Roche Hotel in Paarl. Groups are limited to a maximum of four and trips are held only when the weather permits – in other words, not very often! Tel 863 3192.

# ● beaches

Cape Town is blessed with a liquorice-all-sorts choice of beaches, split between those on the warm Indian Ocean and those along the freezing Atlantic. The trendier beaches are on the Atlantic side, where body exposure is more important than immersion, and they start only a few kilometres from the city centre. Buses and minibus taxis cover the route from the city to Hout Bay and, less frequently, about as far as Muizenberg. The suburban trains practically splash through the surf from Muizenberg to Simon's Town, but check the safety status of your compartment and wrap the Rolex in an old towel before committing yourself to the journey. On both sides of the peninsula, but more so along False Bay, the summer south-east winds can make many beaches a lesson in sandblasting. An early morning tablecloth on Table Mountain is a sure sign of an imminent south-easterly blow. As a general rule, if one side of the peninsula is in the wind, the other side is usually sheltered – but don't bet your mother on it. Working our way along the cold or Atlantic seaboard from the city to Cape Point and around to False Bay, the main beaches are as follows.

## Melkbosstrand

Melkbosstrand is the traditional Christmas beach, complete with boeresport and flabby abs, of the Swartland farming community. It makes for interesting looking on, and at other times there's usually lots of space for walks on this long and attractive beach. Melkbos marks the northern limit of the Cape Town crayfish sanctuary area, a thought that might tempt you into its icy water.

## Bloubergstrand

Bloubergstrand is close to where British troops landed in 1806, to fight the brief battle of Blouberg against the Dutch garrison who inexplicably ignored their own defenses and sallied out to crushing defeat. Blouberg is also known for its surfing and boardsailing at Grootbaai, especially when there's a mild to moderate south-easter blowing, while adjacent Kleinbaai is for swimming. For a postcard view of Cape Town get your bod behind a cocktail at the well-appointed Blue Peter Hotel.

## Milnerton

Milnerton's beach has been discovered by the developers of aesthetically unappealing blocks of flats masquerading as office parks. But north of Woodbridge Island (which happens not to be an island at all), there are still several miles of unspoilt sandy beach much used by the local riding schools and racing stables. Milnerton is excellent kite-flying territory when the south-easter is up and blowing – just about every day in summer.

## Sea Point

A rocky stretch of urban coastline broken by a few patches of sand, Sea Point doesn't have much in the way of a good tanning beach or decent swimming. What does exist tends to be grubby and the water is a potential health hazard. For people-watching though, it can't be beat.

## Clifton

Clifton consists of four smallish beaches that have always been better known for bodies and sundowners than for swimming – dip your big toe into the water and you'll understand why. Bloody right, this is the cold-water side of the peninsula. Blocks of incredibly expensive flats cling to the cliffs overlooking the secluded beaches, and the impression is distinctly Mediterranean. In season impossible parking is part of the penalty, but once you're on the beach nobody can tell whether you arrived by Ferrari or on foot.

## Camps Bay

Camps Bay is an expanded version of Clifton, although not as wind-free, trendy or neat, but with a long rash of amenities – mainly restaurants – along the beachfront. A wide expanse of white sand and lawns stretches from secluded Glen Beach south to a large tidal pool that's usually a bit warmer than the open sea. Saw-tooth peaks make a stunning mountain backdrop that the early settlers called 'de Gevelbergen' or 'gable mountains', now known as the Twelve Apostles. Camps Bay has more parking than Clifton, but there's also a lot more competition. Children and young parents, believed extinct at Clifton, are frequently seen.

## Llandudno

Regulars at this sandy, sheltered beach believe it's worth the almost entire lack of available parking: there's just one road in and the same road out, with a lot of peeved residents in between. Agitation rises with the number of summer visitors and, as at several other peninsula beaches, a barrier is dropped when the road becomes bottlenecked. The white sand and massive granite boulders are perfect for roasting and sundowners, but braving the water needs dedication.

## Sandy Bay

Sandy Bay is the peninsula's original mixed nudie beach, and still prompts a nudge-wink-know-what-I-mean from the more repressed who regularly turn up with their Guide to Coastal Birds. It's the only beach where you can actually see how cold the water is: just watch any bare-bummed hero attempt to enter... Sandy Bay is about 20 minutes' walk from Llandudno – or further if you can't find parking there. Women on their own risk being harassed. Once you've accepted the reservations, it's a cosy place to be, with lots of privacy among the shrubbery.

## Hout Bay

The setting is sensational – specially when approached from Chapman's Peak – and the beach is a wide sandy arc that is safe for swimming. Other than a pleasant stretch of sand, Hout Bay has other attractions, including a genuinely interesting museum, plenty of takeaways and some expanding informal housing. Fairly comfortable launches run daily one-hour cruises to Duiker Island and its seal colony, and are based at the harbour, along with the mild shopping flutter of Mariner's Wharf. (See also page 21 for boat cruise info.)

## Noordhoek

Any beach as big and bold as this one deserves investigation. Despite the sudden dazzle as you drive south from Hout Bay on Chapman's Peak Drive,

Noordhoek attracts relatively few Capetonians. The beach is particularly vulnerable to the south-easter and swimming isn't all that safe. But for a long bracing walk with a quick dip at the end, it's perfect. The tide frequently leaves shallow, warm lagoons and in 1900 it left the brand new freighter Kakapo stranded high and dry – its ribcage still juts forlornly from the sand. Close by are stables that offer beach rides and sunset trails, as well as several pleasant restaurants and coffee shops.

## Kommetjie

Kommetjie got its name from the basin-like tidal pool among the rocks, but serious surfers know it for the winter breaks off Long Beach. For divers there's the prospect of seasonal crayfish pickings in the rocky little bay – and a fat fine if you don't have a licence. Unlike the Hout Bay forests, many of the white milkwoods of Kommetjie survive to offer some shade to pigment-challenged visitors. Some of these trees are centuries old, and the species is strictly protected. Parking is almost always without problems.

## Scarborough

Scarborough Beach is at the end of Camel Rock Road with its caricature rock formation. The adjacent Camel Rock Restaurant (tel 780 1122), open for lunch and dinner, is one of the peninsula's traditional afternoon stops, where generations of locals (starting in 1930), have enjoyed their crayfish delicately done. The sea at Scarborough is for surfing and suicide, but the lagoon at the river mouth is safe and shallow.

## Platboombaai

Within the Cape of Good Hope Nature Reserve, Platboombaai is baboon territory, with a resident troop that will watch your every chew and gesture as you work through your braai. An open car door is an invitation to trash the interior, so take care. Their attachment to Platboom is understandable: sand that really does sparkle (thanks to minute fragments of mica), pristine fynbos, a fair variety of birds and lots of interesting life in the pools. Toilets and fresh water top it off. Bathing is only fair, but not even baboons can have everything.

## Maclear Beach

Maclear Beach is the unlikely haunt of ostriches, usually seen against a background of semi-arid, scrubby Karoo. A rocky shoreline and mountains of kelp are clear indicators of worthwhile diving, but the real attraction of Maclear is the thundering clash of sea and rock, especially at the southern end, where the cliff face is constantly being remodelled. The footpath from the carpark will take you to lonely Dias Beach.

## Cape Point

Cape Point is the most southerly point of the Cape Peninsula (but not of Africa), where steep, ragged cliffs slide easily into the sea. From above, you can watch the sea swirl around Bellows Rock where the liner Lusitania (not the famous one of World War One) was wrecked in 1911 – the lighthouse was built so high up the cliff that it was obscured in fog! Needless to say, the 'new' lighthouse is much nearer sea level. Nearby Dias Beach is small and is usually seen only from the cliff top, but there's a fairly steep path all the way down. The Cape Point viewsite has all the necessary tourism trimmings, including a restaurant and curio shop. For more info dial 780 9100.

## Buffelsbaai

Buffelsbaai is on the False Bay side of Cape Point, in other words the warm side of the peninsula. It is a classic family beach, with shady milkwood trees, grassy picnic sites, safe swimming and baboons.

## Miller's Point

Miller's Point, off the road between Simon's Town and Cape of Good Hope Nature Reserve, has huge, weathered boulders of the granite that forms the basement layer on which the peninsula's surface sandstone was deposited. Their handy exposure provides some shelter from the south-easter. Lawns, several small beaches and pools, and the long-established Black Marlin Restaurant (tel 786 1621) contribute to a summer day well spent.

## Boulders

Boulders is probably the most obviously named beach on the peninsula, and is equally well known for its colony of endangered jackass penguins that are starting to make a numerical comeback despite the occasional battle with villainous oil slicks. Boer prisoners of war, confined to a camp on the present golf course, bathed here 100 years ago. The massive boulders create a sort of Roman bath ambience which adds to the appeal of this beach. A beachfront path links up with Seaforth, with shady lawns, a safe and sheltered little beach, and more boulders.

## Long Beach

Long Beach is the almost endless stretch of sand between the railway line and the surf, running north from Simon's Town railway station. Swimming is good in places (there's also a pool) near the south end. Further along are the very visible remains of the Clan Stuart, blown onto the rocks in 1917. Even today there's no escape from the wind on Long Beach, and no shelter from the sun, but it's great for a really long and peaceful walk and there are plenty of convivial coffee shops and restaurants nearby to while away the hours.

## Fish Hoek

Fish Hoek's status as a 'dry' town is as well known as its magnificent beach. The beach is a long one, although most of the activity is near the southern end, where the swimming is better. On occasions when a shoal of fish is spotted from the shore, you may be lucky enough to see an oared fishing boat put off from the beach, encircle the shoal with its trek net, and then return to pull the hapless catch ashore. Amenities include toilets, fresh water, a restaurant on the beach and an easy walk called Jager (sometimes Jagger) Walk.

## Kalk Bay

Shells were once collected here for burning and making lime (kalk), but today only the name survives. A few traditionalists swim from the tiny beach within the fishing harbour, but a better option is Dalebrook pool and Danger Beach with so-so bathing and no fish-heads. Kalk Bay has a somewhat doll house quality when viewed from the high-level Boyes' Drive, but it's a hard-working fishing harbour, with some of the boat-owners and operators descended from Filipino seamen who settled here in the 1870s. The scene is frantic around mid-year when the snoek are running. The Brass Bell Restaurant (tel 788 5456) on the 'down' platform of the railway station is a Cape Town landmark featuring live music and a copious beer intake. As vibey is the Olympia Café & Deli (tel 788 6396) on Main Road, a brilliant spot for breakfast and late brunch.

### St James

St James is treasured for the large pool, sandy beach and brightly painted cubicles (locally called 'bathing boxes'), all sacred memories and unchanged relics of Cape childhood.

### Muizenberg

Kipling wasn't joking when he warned about 'the white sands of Muizenberg, spun before the gale'. However, this didn't intimidate architect Herbert Baker whose own bijou seaside residence still stands in Beach Road. Mine-owners and empire-builders set up their mansions here too, but fashion has been fickle to Muizenberg and parts of the suburb are in decay. Bathing along this long sandy beach is safe and it's idyllic on calm days. 'Pavilions' as places of seaside entertainment have not really caught on, though in season the hordes queuing for Muizenberg's supertube would tend to disagree. High above Muizenberg is Boye's Drive – a good stretch to pull over and admire the surfer-sprinkled waves marching in straight ranks to the beach.

### Strandfontein

Strandfontein is a continuation of Muizenberg, another gently sloping beach with fairly safe bathing. Sonwabe, Mnandi and Monwabisi are seaside entertainment centres created for the nearby township dwellers.

### Macassar

Macassar is an Oriental name with a history that goes back 300 years, to the arrival of Sheikh Yusuf, a religious and political leader banished by the Dutch from the island of Macassar in the East Indies. His kramat or shrine is one of the holy places of Islam. The beach here shelves too steeply for safe swimming, but you'll always find anglers casting into the surf and beyond.

### Strand

Strand was formerly the Bolanders' annual delight, and probably still is, although most of them seem to have sold their *'strandhuisies'* or beach cottages to high-rise developers with little aesthetic taste. An evening walk from the slipway to the Dynamite Factory fence is a local institution that many visitors also find attractive. Melkbaai, up near the northern end, is the most active section, with boardsailing and hobie-catting. The beach slopes gently so there's lots of shallow water, and there are also several pools. A few bushy dunes offer minimal shelter from the wind, which the local *manne* pretend not to notice if it's anything under Full Gale.

### Gordon's Bay

Gordon's Bay spreads opulently across the mountainside in a fairly sheltered corner of False Bay. The main beach is a kiddies delight of lawn, sand and water that's often so shallow it is a hike just to get your knees wet. Bikini Beach, next to the harbour, shelves more steeply and has rather dumpy waves, but is more sheltered. Numerous milkwood trees survive to shade picnic sites, a seafront walk and some of the parking places. Inevitably, parking can be a problem, but the local authority tries its best. If you aren't going to spend money in their town, the locals prefer you to take the high level road: it's quicker anyway.

# •bead shops

Patronised by kids, hippies, and other featherless magpies, Cape Town's bead shops are the source of a million bohemian accessories. Beads and clasps of every conceivable colour, shape, material and size are sold here – grab a tray and select your favourites. The ancient art of beadstringing offers low-key creative pleasure and dirt-cheap personalised ornamentation. Get into it.

### Bead Sales
Cape Town's original bead shop and still stringing strong after 18 years, Bead Sales have a huge range of beads as well as a selection of ethnic jewellery, inexpensive costume and Indian glass jewellery. 207 Long Street, tel 423 4687, e-mail beadshop@iafrica.com.

### Bead Shop
Tucked up a pretty side street in Claremont, this branch of Bead Sales stocks beads of all shapes, sizes and colours, a range of popular Indian glass bangles and other accessories that will add a sparkle to your t-shirt, matric dance dress or bridal gown. 6 Mark Rd, Claremont, tel 683 2374.

## •birdwatching

Birdwatchers in the Cape are a privileged species. Owing to the presence of coastal habitats and wetlands as well as fynbos, the city's feathered community is fascinatingly diverse. Among the beautiful characters to be spotted are the vlei-dwelling greater flamingo and pelican; and with luck, the magnificent African fish eagle can be seen at work. The fynbos habitat supports over 240 bird species, of which 60 are endemic to South Africa and six endemic to the fynbos zone, including the Cape sugarbird and orange-breasted sunbird. On the coast, birders can watch a teeming commonwealth of gulls, cormorants, terns and more. If quantity is important to you, the Cape of Good Hope Nature Reserve tops the list with 250 species, followed by Rondevlei Nature Reserve at 225 species. So grab the binocs and make like David Attenborough.

### Boulders Beach (Simon's Town)
Pegged somewhere between a fish and *Homo sapiens* on Darwin's evolutionary scale, penguins are the crowd-pleasers of the bird world, providing interest and entertainment to child and adult alike. For a ringside seat head along to Boulders Beach – found a little past Simon's Town – which is one of only two mainland breeding colonies of the African penguin. Nearby is the pleasant Penguin Point Café (tel 786 1758) which offers tasty fare in a relaxed outdoor setting. Boulders Beach, tel 786 2329, open daily 7am-7pm in season (8am-5pm in winter), entry R10 adults, R5 kids.

### Cape of Good Hope Nature Reserve (Cape Point)
Apart from great scenery, a host of other wildlife and a rash of tourist facilities, the reserve tops the Peninsula bird ranks, with a total 250 bird species

## Fairweather Yacht Charters

Fairweather runs a pair of motorised sailing catamarans berthed at the Waterfront's Quay 5. On the menu is a two-hour Table Bay Cruise, a 90-minute Sunset Champagne Cruise and a two-hour Clifton Picnic Cruise, which anchors for lunch off the famous beach. Tel 082-576 4132.

## Maharani

A classic 66-foot ex-naval ketch, the Maharani is billed as "Cape Town's most elegant sailing-ship". Berthed at the Victoria and Alfred Dock at the Waterfront, the Maharani offers cruises to Clifton – with an option to row ashore Robinson Crusoe style – Hout Bay, and around Cape Point to Simon's Town. Tel 082-412 2222, e-mail colinsutcliffe@worldonline.co.za, website www.skynary.com/maharaniyacht.

## Nuisance Express

Named in honour of the South African Navy's legendary canine sailor, Nuisance Express run a Spirit of Just Nuisance cruise around the Simon's Town bay, including a jaunt among strike-craft and submarines in the Navy harbour. Also offered is a 90-minute cruise to Cape Point, and an hour-long trip to Seal Island. Town Pier, Simon's Town, tel 447 2604, cell 083-257 7760, e-mail dhurwitz@iafrica.com.

## Oceanrafters

Oceanrafters challenge you to an invigorating spin around the Atlantic Seaboard in an awesomely powerful motor raft that reaches a speed of 120km/h! The 90-minute trip takes you from the Waterfront to Sandy Bay, Robben Island, Blouberg and back. The worse the weather, the better the ride: wind, spray and a healthy dose of adrenaline are the major ingredients. Tel 425 3785, cell 082-926 2334, e-mail getwet@oceanrafters.co.za, website www.oceanrafters.co.za.

## Steamboat Vicky

A genuine steam-driven passenger ferry berthed at the V&A Dock, Steamboat Vicky takes passengers on a leisurely half-hour cruise around the Waterfront. Good option for kids and those with shaky sea legs. Phone skipper Dave Owen, tel 083-651 0186.

## Sweet Sunshine

A 42-ft sailing catamaran carrying a maximum of 12 passengers, Sweet Sunshine spends its time cruising the False Bay coastline. The menu includes trips to Seal Island and Cape Point, sunset cruises and whale-watching cruises (between August and November). Tel 715 9819, cell 082-575 5655, e-mail sweetsunshine@yebo.co.za, website www.sweetsunshine.co.za.

## Tigger Too Charter Exclusive Cruises

Cruise in style with Tigger Too – a luxurious 40 foot catamaran cruiser kitted out with a bar, spacious interior lounges, sundecks and two cabins. Led by friendly crew, expeditions range between 90-minute sunset cruises and full-day cruises around the Peninsula, all departing from Hout Bay. Crayfish cruises, diving cruises and clay shooting cruises are also offered. Tel 790 5256, cell 082-852 4383, e-mail tigger@netactive.co.za, website www.tiggertoo.co.za.

## Tigresse

The Tigresse is a fast and stylish sailing catamaran berthed at the V&A Waterfront's Quay 5. Cruises take between one and two hours, and explore the coast between Table Bay and Clifton. Tel 419 7746, e-mail robbenis@netactive.co.za.

**Waterfront Adventures**
With Waterfront Adventures you can try anything from a Table Bay cruise aboard the Spirit of Victoria, a 58 foot gaff rigged schooner, to a luxury cruise on a motor yacht with enclosed lounge and sundeck, to a 60-minute jaunt around the harbour aboard a vintage tug. Tel 418 5806, e-mail adventures@dockside.co.za, website www.robben-island.co.za. Present the **Wot to Do Guide** and qualify for a 10% discount on the full ticket price of any cruise.

**Waterfront Charters**
Experience a luxury power catamaran cruise aboard the Sea Princess. Daily trips aboard this and a fleet of other vessels depart from the Pierhead Dock, V&A Waterfront, with Robben Island, Hout Bay, 12 Apostles or a Sunset cruise available on the aquatic itinerary. Tel 418 0134, e-mail sales@waterfrontcharters.co.za, website www.waterfrontcharters.co.za.

# •bo-kaap

The Bo-Kaap, squeezed between the city centre and the slopes of Signal Hill, is a neighbourhood filled with the fragrance of the past. Sometimes called the Malay Quarter, it's been home to the Cape Malay community since the 18th century, when slaves from Indonesia, Sri Lanka and East Africa were brought to the Cape by the Dutch. Unlike District Six, the Bo-Kaap survived apartheid's forced removals policy. The streets are steep, narrow and cobbled, and the house facades display an understated elegance and a subtle mingling of Eastern and Western aesthetics: raised stoeps, simple curvilinear parapets and flat roofs. The Bo-Kaap's most notable building is the beautiful Auwal Mosque on Dorp Street – established in 1798 by Tuan Guru, a Muslim saint and Moluccan prince who guided the emergence of Islam in the Cape as a spiritual antidote to slavery. You can visit the Mosque as part of the official Bo-Kaap Guided Tour (tel 422 1554) – a good option if you're a first-timer to the neighbourhood. Also worth visiting is the Bo-Kaap Museum on 71 Wale Street (tel 424 3846), a national monument which documents the history of the Cape Muslim community.

# •bookshops

Switch off the telly and embark on a journey of daring adventure, exotic cuisine, erotic liaisons, tragic tales and eccentric personalities. Browsing for books, new or secondhand, ranks among life's gentler pleasures, best tailored to a rainy day. The great thing about this activity is you don't even need to buy the merchandise – the crisp touch and sweet smell of a new title, the catchy logos, funky design

like a hapless fish at the end of a line above the lower slopes of Table Mountain. But who needs logic, when your adrenaline-starved brain is screaming out for a fix, your friends are just hanging about waiting to be impressed and you...? You just want to prove to yourself that you can do it. Go ahead, make a date with gravity. But you have to get up early as jumps are only done between 6am to 8am. Face Adrenalin, tel 712 5839, cell 083-264 5221, e-mail extremes@iafrica.com.

**cableway
camel rides
cape point
castle of good hope
caving
classical music
classic car hire
comedy
company gardens
craft markets
cycling**

## •cableway

You have to get to the top of Table Mountain at least once in a while. Now, of course, you can walk up, you could even climb up, but for many it's so much more elegant to do it without sweat. The new cablecars are Cape Town's shiny high tech toy and are everything the old ones weren't – big, sleek and fast, with rotating floors that yield a fish-eye lens of Table Bay, the Atlantic coast, the Hottentots Holland mountains, and the Peninsula. Because the cableway is the most famous tourist attraction in town many tourists and locals shun it as obvious and boring, but it's neither, and opting for a one-way ticket offers the best of two worlds. The nightmare queues of old have been more or less defeated by the newfangled high-speed technology and the revamped upper station offers a smart self-serve restaurant, a bistro and a takeaway, and a shop with a fax and postal facility – why you would want to mail a letter from the top and not the bottom of Table Mountain is an interesting question. Prices vary according to season and status: a student or pensioner taking the popular one-way option in winter pays only R20, while a return trip during high season (Dec-April) will cost an adult R75. Better still, get the edge on the Joneses and buy a Ride 'n Dine ticket which is valid for several weeks and entitles you to one return ticket and either breakfast (R100 adults), lunch or dinner (both R120) at the top of the world. During season, the first car up leaves at 8am, and the last car down leaves at 10pm. The cableway stops running during high winds or bad weather. For more detail phone 424 8181, website www.tablemountain.co.za.

## •camel rides

Once famously described as a horse designed by a committee, the camel is alive and well and giving people joyrides in Cape Town. At Cape Camel Rides, you can perch yourself atop this lumpy oddball beast and parade around the Kommetjie district in true Middle Eastern style. The four camels are harnessed together in caravan formation, and make an hour-long journey through a stretch of bush to Long Beach and back. Shorter rides – 6 minutes and half an hour – are also available. It's not exactly a trans-Sahara trek but a short stint on the back of one of these beasts will convince you that a month-long trek is not quite your cup of tea. (Or perhaps the opposite, of course, in which case next stop Sahara or an audition for the remake of Lawrence of Arabia.) Camel riders are issued with an official Certificate of Bravery. Tel 789 1711, open 12-4pm.

## •cape of good hope nature reserve

This magnificent stretch of veld and coastline, covering the entire southern third of the Cape Peninsula, is virtually unchanged since those quiet centuries when the Khoisan were sole proprietors of the Western Cape. Cape Point, as it is more selectively known among locals, is worth a full day's driving, walking and dreaming. Much of the terrain is an open plain richly decorated with luminous green fynbos, and populated with abundant birdlife, bontebok, eland and baboons. As the reserve traces 40km of rocky coastline it is also a prime spot for whale and dolphin sightings. There are several beautiful and generally deserted beaches to explore, the best of which are Buffelsbaai on the False Bay side and Dias beach on the Atlantic side. The Reserve's major drawcard is, of course, Cape Point itself, a truly majestic promontory overlooking the confluence of two oceans. At the parking lot below the point you can catch a ride up on the funicular (a miniature train), or let your legs do their bit. Allow yourself a good hour on the point – there can be few places as dramatic on this planet. Food is available at the Cape Point Kiosk or Two Oceans Restaurant (tel 780 9200/1), and picnic spots

displays, accompanied by opera and jazz performances. The setting is relaxed, with food, wine and natural splendour close at hand. Off Baden-Powell Drive, en route to Stellenbosch, tel 809 1100, e-mail info@spierarts.org.za, website www.spierfestival.co.za.

## •classic car hire

You're driving through the city on a warm Saturday, and a svelte, gleaming, convertible pulls up alongside you at a traffic light. Assuming you yourself don't possess such a vehicle, how do you perceive the person behind the wheel? A jerk, a symptom of the owner's sexual inadequacy? But that's just because you're jealous! Beautiful cars, especially old ones, are categorically cool and the good news is, you needn't actually buy one to experience the Cape's suitably spectacular roads. Instead, hire a classic car for a day or two, and enter a temporary James Bond dreamworld made of glamour, rubber, freedom and chrome.

### Cape Cobra Car Hire

Original Cobras are rare as hen's teeth, but from Cape Cobra you can rent a magnificent replica fitted with a Chevy 5.7 litre V8 engine, Jaguar suspension and brakes, leather interior and detachable soft top. It's a powerful vehicle for its weight, so take it real easy. Tel 531 1542, cell 082-564 1617, e-mail hilton@apple-group.co.za.

### Classic Twin Tours

Original early 1970's MG convertibles can be hired from Classic Twin Tours. These profoundly stylish cars come in blue, black, white and yellow. Antique Tractor Guest House, Koelenhof, Stellenbosch (R304), tel 882 2558, e-mail enquiries@classictwintours.com, website www.classictwintours.com.

## •comedy

In a city and a world in which the only alternative to laughter is chronic weeping, many are turning to hysterical cackling as a full-time occupation. A lunatic generation of young stand-up comics have sprouted to serve this growing market – and chewing on their sweet-and-sour gags is now a fashionable and refreshing way to spend an evening. Locally-based jesters to watch out for are Mark Lottering, David Levinson, Chris McEvoy, David Kau, Mark Sampson and Irit Noble. Of the upcountry crew who periodically take the piss in the Mother City, veteran Mel Miller, Mark Banks and John Vlismas are well worth lending an ear.

**The Cape Comedy Collective**
The CCC showcases the town's top mic rats and nurtures new standup talent. Its weekly Sunday night shows at the Independent Armchair Theatre in Observatory (tel 447 1514) have been the springboard for a string of fine young comics and continue to attract buzzing crowds. The CCC also presents a Hardcore night for insensitive comics and patrons with insensitive dispositions at the Purple Turtle (cnr Long & Shortmarket St) as well as a number of other regular shows at venues across the city. Tel 447 1023, website www.comedyclub.co.za.

## • company gardens

A smallish but gratifying green lung in the centre of Cape Town, the Company Gardens were planted in 1652 for the purpose of supplying lettuce to queasy, scurvy-stricken Dutch sailors. By the end of the 17th century the veggies were turfed out in favour of oak trees, lawns and flowers, and people have been strolling and canoodling along the shady cobbled walkways ever since. In the Gardens you'll find a fountain prowled by obese carp, an outdoor restaurant, an aviary and enough grey squirrels to cause a global peanut shortage. There's a statue of Cecil John Rhodes pointing pompously northwards – it was while walking in the Gardens that he hit on the bright idea of conquering present-day Zimbabwe. If you're after some indoor diversions, the South African Library, the National Gallery, the SA Museum and the Holocaust Museum are all in close proximity, while the Tuynhuys and the Houses of Parliament are on the opposite side of Government Avenue.

## • craft markets

Craft markets and flea markets are definitely not one and the same species – Roleks watches, Nikey running shoes and Gutchi faux leather bags tend to be stock fare at flea markets, while at authentic craft markets you will find a vast range of handmade goods, some brilliant, others of questionable practical or aesthetic use. Squeeze into your favourite tie-dye T-shirt, tuck into a boerewors roll and hit the craft market circuit – apart from meeting people that are doing it for themselves you'll find the experience a healthy and refreshing break from your usual mass consumption mall prowlings.

### Constantia Market
A regular on the craft market circuit that takes place on the first and last Saturday (and the first Sunday), of the month. On display are a variety of goodies that are exclusively handcrafted and usually made and sold by the very individual standing before you. You'll find everything from scarves to

mac towards Llandudno. At the Llandudno turnoff, either turn back or commit yourself to Hout Bay and back, or if really up to it, onward to Chapman's Peak (when open) and Noordhoek for breakfast. No lack of options but the question is: Is your bod up for the challenge?

**day trips
diving
drumming**

## •day trips

Life in the city getting a little cramped lately? If so, maybe it's a good time to venture further afield into a refreshing world of vineyards, gabled homesteads, cavorting whales, snowy peaks and wide open plains. There's nothing like a road trip to refuel the senses and instil a sense of appreciation of all things local and lekker. Cape Town's satellite suburbs, Stellenbosch, Franschhoek, Hermanus, Darling and others, are all within an easy hop and skip from the city centre and each has something different to share, something different to add, to your life's kaleidoscopic mosaic. Fill the tank, adjust the shades and escape into the wide yonder.

### Franschhoek

Franschhoek likes to be known for its French image, wine and culinary delights. The valley is stunning and although the town itself falls somewhat short of the mini-Stellenbosch one might expect, it's clearly thriving on the attention shown by foreign tour buses and local visitors. Timed for a late winter or bonny spring day the valley is an idyllic day trip filled with gorgeous vistas, sumptuous food and flowing wine.

Many head out to Franschhoek for the sole purpose of indulging their taste buds. The town has fashioned itself as the gourmet capital of the Cape and every building that isn't a guesthouse or antique shop is a restaurant. Of the 20 or so establishments dotted along the main drag, many are excellent and expensive, others just plain expensive – so choose carefully.

Franschhoek's other great drawcard is its wine estates, or 'Vignerons de Franschhoek' as the wine route prefers to be called. Fourteen of the 19 estates are open to the public, among them the ever popular Boschendal, which boasts 18th century Cape Dutch elegance, beautiful gardens, a good restaurant and an al fresco picnic under scented pine trees. Other than the Cape Dutch architecture of the surrounding estates, Franschhoek itself has few buildings of great historical interest. On your stroll through the village however, you may like to pop into the Huguenot Monument and Museum, depicting the French influence on the area.

While few head to Franschhoek for hardcore physical pursuits the adjacent La Motte Plantation, a scenic milieu of dense pine, cascading streams and dramatic mountain and valley views, harbours long walks, horse and mountain bike trails. Close by is the farm Robertsvallei (tel 876 2160), which offers horse trails and an opportunity to pit your wits against a stubborn creature with bad teeth.

Franschhoek in the bag and an extra inch on the waistline, returning home via Villiersdorp is a pleasant alternative, stopping along the scenic Franschhoek Pass to watch the African sun dip into the horizon's penny slot. For more info contact the Franschhoek Tourism Office, tel 021-876 3603.

## Stellenbosch

Stellenbosch is the undisputed heartbeat of the Cape winelands. Home to gracious homesteads, 300-year-old oak avenues, towering mountains, the country's oldest wine route and a good selection of restaurants, the town is at its traditional best on a bonny Sunday – the rest of the week is a little frenetic. Stellenbosch is a quick 45-minute drive from Cape Town and even if you don't have your own vehicle, you can get there easily by train.

Stellenbosch seeps with heritage and the best way to acquaint yourself with three centuries of turbulent past, is on foot. Armed with a map and a heap of brochures – pick these up at the Info office on Market Street – a good place as any to start your tour is Dorp Street. The oldest avenue in town, Dorp has a higher concentration of historical monuments than any other in the country, with buildings dating back as far as 1710. At one end of the road, crammed with bric and brac, traditional food and other weird and wonderful country fare, is Oom Samie se Winkel – Stellenbosch's oldest surviving trading store and still going strong. Close by is the gabled Rembrandt van Rijn Art Museum housing works by Irma Stern, William Kentridge and other notable South African artists, while other historic buildings include the Theological College, the Old Parsonage and the Old Lutheran Church. Up Dorp and left into Ryneveld Street will bring you to the Village Museum which comprises four adjacent houses, the Shreuderhuis, Blettermanhuis, Grosvenor House and Bergh House, each meticulously preserved and dating from different periods between 1709 and 1803. The Museum is an absorbing insight to the historical shifts in architectural and cultural sensibility.

Once you've had your fill of culture, you may like to turn to more hedonistic or physical pursuits. There's a convenient selection of restaurants, coffee shops and student watering holes dotted about town, suited to a range of budget, palate and social temperament. Either dine in the centre itself or hold back for the wine estates. Blaauwklippen, Delaire, Morgenhof and Spier are all within 7km of Stellenbosch and offer good options.

A few kilometres out of town is Jonkershoek Nature Reserve, among the country's most beautiful valleys – a setting of scented fynbos and fern-lined kloofs punctuated by a towering wall of rock and the Jonkershoek Twins. Mountain biking in the plantation and several mapped hikes in the valley's upper reaches are available with a permit, which you can buy at the gate. Cars are allowed on the pleasant circular drive which has several informal picnic spots along a gurgling stream. Across town, the Vineyard Trail offers more foot- and pedal-slogging but on sheer beauty pales alongside Jonkershoek.

With close to 70 estates and co-ops the Stellenbosch wine route is nothing short of daunting but fortunately not all are open to the public. Those that are tend to close shop around 1pm Saturday and re-open Monday morning. Perhaps go for the smaller estates which cater less to tour buses and more to personal service. And of course, don't try cover all estates in one

Atlantic while in winter you're likely to find yourself in the warmer waters of False Bay. Either way you'll have a lot of fun! Visit Sarah, Barry or Pam at 22 Carlisle St, Paarden Eiland, tel 511 0800/15, cell 082-881 1660, e-mail diveact@iafrica.com, website http://come.to/diveaction. Show the **Wot to Do Guide** and qualify for a 5% discount on course prices or 10% on gear sales!

### Dive Junction
Dive Junction offer one-day resort dives as well as "aqua-adrenalin" dives in the company of ragged-toothed sharks in the predators' tank at the Two Oceans Aquarium. Tel 511 7760, e-mail jurg@lando.co.za, website www.divejunction.co.za.

### Dusky Dive Academy
You can join Dusky Dive for a one-day Naui-affiliated resort course including a pool tutorial and a 6m ocean dive. All equipment is provided, and you'll be taken to wrecks or reefs on either coast according to seasonal conditions. If you complete the weeklong beginners' course, Dusky Dive will give you 10 free airfills for future adventures. c/o Alpinist Outdoor, 33 Castle St, Cape Town, tel 426 1622, e-mail alpinist@netactive.co.za.

### Far Side Adventures
Far Side offers passport dives on both sides of the Peninsula, depending on water conditions. They specialise in wreck diving and technical diving. 66 St George's St, Simon's Town, tel 786 2599, e-mail farside@iafrica.com, website www.farside.co.za.

### Table Bay Diving
Wreck dives, reef dives, night dives, shore dives and seal dives, Table Bay Diving offers these and more. Also on offer from this Waterfront-based outfit are a number of courses, from PADI to Dive Master. Everyone, from novice to experienced frogman is welcome. Tel 419 1780, e-mail condor@iafrica.com.

### Want to know more?
Completely updated and revised, the *Globetrotter Dive Guide South Africa: Over 180 Top Dive and Snorkel Sites* (Struik New Holland Publishing), is an indispensable intro to diving and snorkelling in local waters, pitched at enthusiasts at all levels of expertise.

## •drumming

Hitting a djembe or darbuka drum with your bare hands is one of the most gratifying activities known to humanity. Hand drumming is therapeutic, expressive and sociable. It's a compulsory hobby among Cape Town's floating population of hippies – but you don't have to be a hirsute New Age nomad to get a kick out of making a racket. Do it on a mountaintop or on a beach, or link up with fellow beat freaks at a dedicated drum evening.

**The Drum Café**
The Drum Café is a nightclub committed to the pleasures of percussion: on weeknights you can hire a drum and join a communal session co-ordinated by experienced djembe drummers. Beginners are most welcome – so don't feel shy. A typical week at the Drum Café is filled with drum workshops, interactive open drum circles and laid-back evenings washed by the jazzy sounds of West Africa. 32 Glynn St, Gardens, tel 462 1064, e-mail anthonybank@hotmail.com, website www.drumcafe.co.za, open Mon, Wed, Fri, Sat (Sun in season).

## fly-fishing

Standing knee deep in a crystal mountain pool, watching a trout rise on the current and, with a soft "blip", intercept your fly. Can't imagine anything more soothing or thrilling, can you? The gentle art of fly-fishing may not be as easy as it first appears but the rewards are great and well worth the initial effort. A few hours on a field should get your casting up to pretty reasonable, and then you just need to obtain a permit, a bunch of flies, a bottle of Glenfiddich and a map of the hills. (Oh, and a rod, some of those big green waders, a ridiculous hat and one of those waistcoats with bits of fluff on it, will also help.) If you've never tried this before, it's best to go with an experienced guide – someone who knows how to get woolly buggers out of trees.

**Ultimate Angling**
A hazy dawn, casting to a wild trout rising through crystal waters... A scene from A River Runs Through It? Actually no, it's a day in the life of Tim Rolston, local fly-fishing aficionado and experienced guide who is willing to share this enviable lifestyle with you. Ultimate Angling offers casting clinics and guided fishing trips to some of the best trout water in the Cape, with all tackle and transport provided. Get dialling. Tel 686 6877, cell 083-6260467, e-mail rolston@iafrica.com, website www.durandel.co.za/flyfishsa.

**Want to know more?**
Dean Riphagen's *The South African Fly-fishing Handbook* (Struik New Holland Publishing) is a teach yourself approach to this gentle art. Step by step instructions, more than 500 photographs, tips from the masters and fly-fishing anecdotes provide a solid introduction. Another good point of entry is *The Honda Book on Fundamental Fly-fishing Techniques for Southern Africa* (B2 Marketing CC). Buying the right equipment, tying a decent knot, preparing your lines, where to fish and how to cast are among

karting. For the repressed speed freak this is happiness itself: a miniature replica of a professional racecourse, chunky fat-tired go-karts that are like lawnmowers on Viagra, and a computerised timing system that precisely ranks you and your fellow karter's times after the race. The fever of Formula One will inflame your soul. You will crash. You won't get hurt. You will overtake. You will grin from ear to ear.

### Indoor Grand Prix
Arrive and drive this high speed circuit on the Foreshore. Prices range between R30 for 15 laps to R50 for 40 laps. Cool off after burning rubber at the adjacent pub. Coen Steytler Building, V&A Waterfront, tel 419 5465, e-mail indoorgp@mweb.co.za, website www.indoorkarting.co.za, open daily 11.30am-11.30pm (longer over weekends).

### Kenilworth Karting
A popular track for Lauda wannabes and corporate groups. Kids can let rip on the under 10's Junior racetrack while adult karters are charged R20 for 20 laps and R40 for 40 laps. Like the Indoor Grand Prix there is a pub attached for after action satisfaction. 10 Myhof Rd, Kenilworth, tel 683 2670, e-mail kenilworthkarting@karting.co.za, open daily until 11pm (opening times vary), but phone ahead to ensure track availability.

## •golf-driving ranges

If you're one of the growing community of otherwise reasonable people who spend their free time getting a little white ball into a distant little hole by means of a bucket of sticks, Cape Town is well-suited to your needs. Golfers and golf courses abound – but if you feel a sudden urge to polish your putting or doctor your drive, drop in at a driving range and whack some balls.

### The Golf Academy
At the Golf Academy in Durbanville you can hone your skills on a driving range, a chipping facility and putting greens, as well as a 9-hole pitch and putt course. Clubs can be hired, and one-off professional coaching is available, as are drinks and takeaways. Eversdal Rd, Durbanville, tel 981 6042, e-mail golfacad@iafrica.com, driving range open daily 9am-6pm, 9-hole course 9am-7pm.

### Peninsula Golf Driving Range
You can play off grass – as opposed to the usual plastic matting – at the modest Peninsula Golf Driving Range. Clubs are for hire, and expert coaches can be enlisted to fine-tune your swing. Revenues are donated to school feeding schemes. Alexander Rd, Maitland, tel 511 1934, open daily 9am-5pm (6pm in summer).

### The River Club
A huge building with a huge driving range in its backyard, the River Club incorporates The Pro-Shop, purveyors of golf gear, and the River Club Golf

Academy which offers expert tutoring on request. Among the River Club's features are putting greens, a chipping facility and a double-decker driving tee. Buy a bucket of balls, hire some clubs if you need to, and get swinging. A full bar, pool tables and a decent restaurant can be found inside. Observatory Road, Observatory (off Liesbeek River Parkway), tel 448 6117, e-mail academy@riverclub.co.za, open 9am-9pm weekdays, Sat-Sun 9am-7pm.

## •greenmarket square

Greenmarket Square is Cape Town's humming spiritual hub, an old and intimate place dedicated to the fine arts of browsing, sunsoaking, chatting, and trying on hippie sandals. In years past, the cobbled Square has been a slave market, a fresh produce market, and a parking lot – but now it's home to a fragrant labyrinth of stalls selling crafts, clothing, jewellery, music, books and textiles. The market is surrounded by Art Deco and Cape Dutch buildings and pavement coffee shops serenaded by buskers and street performers. In the height of summer, the Square becomes a multihued beehive, crawling with *Homo shopiens* – drop by on a sunny winter day and you'll have a less chaotic experience. Shortmarket St, Cape Town, market open Mon-Sat.

**helicopter flips**
**horseriding**
**hout bay**

## •helicopter flips

What with fighting fires, watching traffic and rescuing people, most helicopters have precious little time for frivolous pursuits. But a select few choppers are a touch decadent, and can be hired for a breathtaking spin around the Cape Peninsula. A "heliflip", as it is known, is a superb opportunity to admire mountain, sea, and city from the air. Get a bunch of people together and get a new perspective on everything. The rotors make a bit of a racket, but that's also kinda cool.

**Civair**
On offer from Civair is a 20-minute Two Bay tour – from the Waterfront to Hout Bay and back – and the 30-minute Two Ocean tour which adds Kalk Bay and Muizenberg to the route. The hour-long Full Peninsula tour goes all the way to Cape Point. Tel 419 5182, e-mail civair@mweb.co.za, website www.civair.co.za.

### Ingwe Africa Helicopter Charters
Ingwe Africa offers a choice of three heliflips, all departing from and returning to the Waterfront. The 20-minute Atlantico flight circles the City Bowl and soars over the top of Table Mountain. The Two Oceans flight lasts 30 minutes and includes the Atlantic seaboard, the False Bay Coast, and the Constantia winelands. To The Point is a full hour, that takes you all the way to Cape Point and back. Tel 418 3444, e-mail ingwe@iafrica.com.

### Sport Helicopters
Taking off from the V&A Waterfront, Sport Helicopters have a package of popular standard flights, ranging from 15 to 60 minutes in the air, taking in the beauty of the Atlantic coastline to the isolated drama of Robben Island. Or better still, for a flip with a difference, touch down at a wine estate and enjoy admiring glances and a sumptuous luncheon. Tel 419 5907/8, cell 082-491 7905, e-mail info@sport-helicopters.co.za.

## •horseriding

For some, the horse is the noblest beast ever to roam the planet; for others it is an oversized, bad-tempered organic bicycle. Decide for yourself by saddling up and joining a horseriding expedition in the spacious setting of the Noordhoek valley, the Ottery farmlands or the Cape vineyards. The emphasis is on leisurely walking, spiced up by the occasional trot and a canter or two.

### Horse Trail Safaris
Horse Trail Safaris offer an hour-long ride through rural Ottery, a 90-minute ride through dune country to Strandfontein beach, and a full-day ride along the False Bay coast with lunch included. The equine staff include thoroughbreds, Arabs and *boerperde*, all responsive and amenable. Weekend and longer trails in the Cape hinterland are also offered. Indicator Lodge, Schaapkraal Rd, Ottery, tel 703 4396.

### Imhoff Farm Horse Rides
Imhoff Farm offers two-hour beach rides, bush rides, sunset rides and champagne breakfasts. Light lunches are provided, and riding lessons for all are offered. All the horses are specially selected to match the stubbornness of their riders. Tel 783 1168, cell 082-774 1191.

### Sleepy Hollow Horse Riding
Sleepy Hollow's outings take six riders at a time to Noordhoek beach, the wreck of the Kakapo, and the bird-rich Noordhoek Wetlands. Lessons are also available. Tel 789 2341, cell 083-261 0104.

### Wine Valley Horse Trails
Explore the gorgeous Winelands on horseback with this experienced and friendly outfit based near Paarl. Wine Valley Horse Trails offers a number of packages suited to beginner and pro alike and to all hours of the day, from a leisurely champagne breakfast trail to wine tasting and sundowner trails. Saddle time ranges from three to six hours, and with two proficient guides always on hand, both the bumpety-bump slow rider and those practising for the Derby are catered for. Tel 863 8687, cell 083-226 8735, e-mail gavmic@worldonline.co.za.

# hout bay

With a superb setting and a rash of tourist amenities, Hout Bay has for long been a consistent crowd-puller. The bay may no longer be the quaint fishing and rural outpost it once was – the forests that gave the place its name (hout = wood) were chopped out long ago and formal and informal development across the valley is rife – but it has many other attractions, most centred around water and fish. The harbour and Mariner's Wharf, the country's first stab at harbourfront emporiums, is the focal point for most visitors – a mini V&A Waterfront with seafood restaurants, greasy takeaways, curio shops and a fish market. Fairly comfortable launches run daily one-hour cruises to Duiker Island and its seal colony, with regular departures from the harbour (see page 21). Seafood and especially snoek in various forms is the local cashcrop and actively promoted: try it if you aren't on a salt-free diet. Near the harbour is Hout Bay's beach – a wide arc of sand that's safe for swimming but somewhat crowded over season. For a flashback to how things were in the good old days, before the developers and migrant workers arrived, the Hout Bay Museum in Andrews Road is a genuinely interesting experience. As interesting and probably a lot more entertaining for a family outing is World of Birds on Valley Road. With over 330 species fluttering overhead, Alfred Hitchcock would love it, those suffering from feather allergy perhaps not (see page 121).  Hout Bay Info, tel 790 3270.

ice-skating

# ice-skating

Owing to pleasant weather and liquid waterways, ice-skating is not a widespread sport in South Africa. Some Capetonians have developed a serious passion for ice despite this, and the rink is their oyster. Most visitors are casual skaters, however, and local ice rinks tend to see more in the way of slapstick collisions than elegant pirouettes. Skating is about glamour, romance, comedy and cold, bruised butts. Find out for yourself at the all-new Ice Station, housed in the mammoth Grand West Casino Complex at Century City. Tel 535 2260, open daily (times vary), entry R15 per session with own boots, R20 including boot hire.

# J

jetskiing

## • jetskiing

Jetskiing brings the macho thrill of big bikes into the spiritually invigorating arena of the ocean. Riding this fast, funky vessel through the wind and sparkling surf may lead you to believe that you've been reincarnated as an extra in a cigarette commercial. Worse things have happened. Jetskis are safe, easy to manoeuvre and they make you grin a lot. Advance booking is advisable: instruction, wetsuits and lifejackets are provided by operators.

### Rent 'n Ride
A friendly hire shop near the lighthouse in Mouille Point that, apart from mountain bikes and roller-blades offers a jetski rental service. Place R350 on the table and the ocean is your oyster for a delirious 60 minutes. 1 Park Rd, Mouille Point, tel 434 1122, e-mail bahamab@iafrica.com, open 10am to sunset.

### Wetbikes Cape Town
Operating from Blouberg and Granger Bay near the Waterfront, Wetbikes has five jetskis for hire (GP 800s) and a rubber duck equipped with waterskis. Various jetski packages are available, from a 30-minute spin around the bay to a full day of wet thrill and spill. Tel 551 3988, cell 083-655 2266.

### Yellow Submarine
Another outfit working off Granger Bay, Yellow Submarine has a six-pack of powerful jetskis, available for hire at R350 per hour. Life jackets, wetsuits and an introduction to the art of serious fun are included in the price. Tel 083-524 5995, open 7 days a week.

# K

kayaking
kirstenbosch
kite-flying
kite-surfing
kloofing

## • kayaking

The Eskimos achieved a masterstroke of functional design with the kayak, a slender little paddle boat that became the Vespa of the Arctic Ocean. The contemporary model is ultra-light with a day-glo paint job, and you'd be hard pressed to find a more pleasurable way of amusing yourself in Cape Town waters. Whether you're braving choppy seas or cruising lazily across a silent sun-kissed vlei, the kayak is a cheap ticket to enlightenment.

### Aquatrails

Introducing a novel concept in marine adventure: the inflatable Croc – until recently only spotted in river water. This two-man Lazy-Boy of the open sea is safe, loads of fun and far easier to balance than your traditional kayak or surf ski. For an enjoyable introduction, join Aquatrails for a paddle along the picturesque Atlantic or False Bay coastline. Aquatrails have been satisfying water rats for about fifteen years, so you can be sure of a good time. Tel 762 7916, e-mail aquatrails@mweb.co.za, website www.aquatrails.co.za.

### Cape Sport Centre Kayak Rental

Hire a quality kayak from Cape Sport Centre and explore the placid expanse of Langebaan Lagoon. Guided day trips in and around the Lagoon are also offered. Langebaan, tel 022-772 1114, cell 082-658 1114, e-mail cwsa@iafrica.com, website www.capesport.co.za.

### Real Cape Adventures

Discover SA's magnificent marine heritage with this friendly local outfit. Real Cape runs guided kayak trips off Sea Point, Hout Bay, Simon's Town, Boulders and up the West Coast and Garden Route. For the very experienced paddler, there is even an epic Cape Point route. The routes are graded to suit different levels of ability, and training and all equipment are provided. Tel 790 5611, cell 082-556 2520, website www.seakayak.co.za, e-mail johan@mweb.co.za.

### Want to know more?

Multitalented Johan Loots of Real Cape Adventures has written two comprehensive books on the subject of kayaking. *A Practical Guide to Sea Kayaking in Southern Africa* (Struik New Holland Publishing) is packed with info that both the beginner and seasoned pro will find useful. Equipment, basic paddling skills, safety and a comprehensive overview of 50 of the sub-continent's prime sea kayaking routes are covered. From the same pen comes *Sea Kayaking: The Essential Guide to Equipment and Techniques* (New Holland Publishers – UK), a useful technical introduction to the pleasurable sport.

# •kirstenbosch national botanical garden

One of the world's greatest botanical gardens, Kirstenbosch is an enthralling monument to South Africa's oxygen-producing citizens. A dizzying range of admirable plants cohabit in Kirstenbosch's cultivated gardens, which include a cycad amphitheatre, a protea and erica garden, a fragrance garden and a hardworking community of 'Useful Plants'. A climate-controlled conservatory is home to bizarre and beautiful succulents, ferns, and bulbs. The Garden's rolling lawns, incomparable views of Table Mountain make it a prime dreaming-and-loafing spot. And with a rash of comfortable amenities, including three restaurants – a self-serve eatery, a coffee shop, and a formal sitdown with starched linen and a fairly creative menu – even the querulous gourmet from Hamburg should be satisfied. A number of short and longer trails fan out from the cultivated gardens into the adjacent forest and fynbos and up Table Mountain. Kirstenbosch also hosts immensely popular jazz and classical concerts on summer Sunday afternoons; watch the press for details. Rhodes Drive, Newlands, tel 799 8899, website www.nbi.co.za, open daily, 8am-6pm winter, 8am-7pm summer, entrance R15 adults, R5 kids.

## •kite-flying

It's an artful sport – or is it a sporty art? Kite-flying has enchanted millions since it was pioneered in ancient China, and the wide blustery beaches of the Cape make for consummate kite terrain. Whether you're dancing with a rustic dowl-and-paper diamond or a bells-and-whistles dual-line powerkite, the principle remains the same: enter the kite's mind, relish the pulse of the wind in your arms, and soar into a waking dream. The prime kiting spots are Dolphin Beach in Blouberg and Noordhoek beach, but anywhere with sky, space and a stiff breeze will do.

### The Kite Shop
An amazing range of imported and locally-made kites are on sale at the Kite Shop. For advice and a demonstration of advanced kite-flying, catch the Kite Shop's experts at Dolphin Beach on Saturdays and most weekday late afternoons. 110 Victoria Wharf Shopping Centre, Waterfront, tel 421 6231, e-mail kiteshop@iafrica.com, website www.kiteshop.co.za.

## •kite-surfing

It's the latest bright idea in the field of watersports philosophy, and kite-surfing is attracting enthusiasts by the minute. The board you stand on is akin to a wakeboard (but the sport is still in its infancy and the design is evolving all the time) and the kite that propels you across the water and yanks you into the air is fitted with special bubbles to stay afloat when it hits the surface. Kite-surfing is as ingenious as a Leonardo Da Vinci contraption and exceptionally funky. What more do you need?

### Cape Sport Centre
At Cape Sport Centre in Langebaan, you can get expert kite-surfing tuition and rent easy-to-use Naish kites and boards for an hour or a full day. The

consistent wind and clean, flat water of the Langebaan Lagoon make it one of the finest kite-surfing venues anywhere. Tel 022-772 1114, e-mail cwcsa@iafrica.com, website www.capesport.co.za.

# • kloofing

The rivers that spring from the Western Cape's mountainous heights are decorated with astounding rock formations, waterfalls of many shapes and sizes, and rock pools deep enough to dunk a giraffe in. The best way to enjoy all this is to spend a day kloofing: hike to the top of a gorge, then follow the river's course downwards, clambering from rock to rock and leaping into pools as they appear. Vertigo sufferers need not apply – jumps can vary from 5m to a heart-thumping 18m and more. If you're fairly fit and you like making a splash, this is an outdoor adventure with few rivals.

### Abseil Africa

Join Abseil Africa for a day packed with adrenaline and high adventure in the magnificent Kamikaze Kanyon. After a bumper breakfast and a short hike into the belly of the gorge you're ready to go. Start with a baby leap of 3m, build up to 10m and then, face the monster of them all, a 22m blood-curdling plunge into the black pools below. The day climaxes with a 65m slither down Thunderfalls, among the Cape's best abseils. Adventure Village, 229B Long St, tel 424 1580, e-mail thrills@adventure-village.co.za, website www.adventure-village.co.za.

### Day Trippers

Kloofing expeditions with Day Trippers take place on Tuesdays and Fridays, leaving Cape Town soon after sunrise and back home in time to watch Days of Our Lives. The full package fee of around R325 includes transport, two competent guides, permits, lunch and post-trip beer and snacks. 8 Pineway, Pinelands, tel 531 3274, cell 082-807 9522, e-mail trippers@iafrica.com, website www.daytrippers.co.za.

live music

# • live music

Ever since Urk banged two rocks together and then passed around a stone hat, people have been paying hard cash to watch other people make a noise. When the music is good, there is something magically luxurious and intimate about a live musical performance, a fluid immediacy that no amount of sci-fi sound technology can displace. Cape Town is an excellent place to develop a hardcore gig addiction: it's home to several live-music cultures, from African jazz and goema to hip hop, rock, reggae, traditional percussion, gothic metal, gospel and skate-punk. (There is even a skate-punk gospel scene in Bellville.) The summer season sees a tasty influx of upcountry bands playing live in the city, while every so often an African superstar will drop into town. Keep your eyes (and ears) peeled.

The city is one of the world's **jazz** capitals, having produced maestros such as the internationally acclaimed pianist Abdullah Ibrahim and the legendary trio of saxophonists Basil "Mannenberg" Coetzee, Winston "Ngozi" Mankunku and Robbie Jansen. The jazz sound they pioneered is a hypnotic, melodic and hair-raisingly emotional fusion of American, African and Cape Malay idioms. Mankunku and Robbie Jansen play club gigs on occasion; keep an eye on the press. Younger additions to the city's jazz Hall of Fame are the ultra-cool guitar ace Jimmy Dludlu, the subtle and mellow pianist Paul Hanmer, the superbly vibrant singer Judith Sephuma. Also watch out for guitarists Errol Dyers and Selaelo Selota, bassist Spencer Mbadu and Jo'burg-based stars like pianist Moses Molelekwa, saxman McCoy Mrubata and bassist Sipho Gumede. If any of these people can be heard live, they categorically should not be missed.

The popularity of electronic music among Cape Town youth has taken some of the sting out of the city's **rock** circuit. But the best of the city's rock bands are bucking the trend and packing out venues with charismatic live performances. Boland-reared art-rockers the Springbok Nude Girls are developing a more exciting and anthemic sound with every recording, while the dark epic blues crafted by Fetish promises to bring them international acclaim. For a lighter touch, seek out the tightly crafted melodic pop of The Usual. One of the best live acts around is the boereblues legend Valiant Swart and his band.

The local **hip-hop** scene is growing up. While the original Cape Flats crew Prophets of Da City rarely play live, fellow pioneers Black Noize and Brasse vannie Kaap take the mic with some regularity. Don't miss the talented soul/hip-hop collective Moodphase 5ive.

### Café Camissa

Cosy and studiedly laid-back, Café Camissa is one of the best hangouts on Kloof Street. To fully savour its charms, settle into a window table with a game of Jenga, and let a sun-drenched city afternoon seep past you. By night Camissa is always buzzing, with low-key live music to be enjoyed on Wednesday and Sunday evenings. 80 Kloof St, Gardens, tel 424 2289, open 11am till late daily.

### Dizzy Jazz Café
A busy nightspot with outdoor tables, good draught beer and a crack of sea view. Live jazz can be caught on Fridays and Saturdays; the rest of the week expect to be wooed with live band sounds from Africa through to mainstream. 41 The Drive, Camps Bay, tel 438 2686.

### Drum Café
For a pulsating bout of rhythmic recreation, drink a beer and beat a hired drum at the Drum Café. The communal drumming sessions hosted here are sometimes enthralling, sometimes just a godawful racket. If you'd rather leave the mother of all instruments to the experts – percussion and African bands enter the spotlight several nights a week. Light meals are available. 32 Glynn St, Gardens, tel 462 1064, e-mail anthonybank@hotmail.com, website www.drumcafe.co.za, open Mon, Wed, Fri, Sat (Sun in season).

### Gignet Theatre Café
A new supper club/bar (previously The Edge) on the live music and cabaret scene featuring the eclectic likes of the Glen Robertson Band, Virtual Jazz Reality, The Rockets, Marc Lottering, Tina Schouw and a host of other upcoming crooners. 67/69 Buitengracht St, Cape Town, tel 424 6550, e-mail infotheatrecafe@gignet.co.za, website www.gignet.co.za, open daily.

### Green Dolphin
A blue-chip jazz venue, with seafood on the menu and a packed schedule of first-rate jazz combos. Jazz evenings are held seven days a week, kicking off at 8pm. The cover charge is R15 for an out-of-sight window table, R20 if you want to see the musos in action. Victoria and Alfred Pierhead, tel 421 7471, e-mail green-dolphin@mweb.co.za, website www.greendolphin.co.za.

### Harbour Music Club
A platform for upcoming and established local acoustic musos, among them Robin Auld and members of the Aquarian Quartet (Steve Newman, Tony Cox), the Harbour Music Club hosts a line-up of about four gigs every week at Kalk Bay's Troubadour. The club is a labour of love – except for two free drinks and public exposure the musicians receive no perks. A bar and reasonably priced food are available. The Troubadour, 17 Johns Rd, Kalk Bay, tel 789 1021, gigs held Wednesdays at 8.30pm, R15 entry; alternatively buy an annual membership for R50 and commit your ears to a worthy music cause.

### Independent Armchair Theatre
Generously furnished with several lounge suites, The Independent Armchair Theatre offers physical comforts and high-quality live entertainment. A steady stream of notable jazz, rock and avant-garde bands play here, while cult films are screened on week nights. Comedy nights happen every Sunday from 8pm – extremely well-attended, so get there early for a good seat and a chance to be picked on. 135 Lower Main Rd, Observatory, tel 447 1514.

### The Jam
A roomy and adventurous venue which showcases quality rock and hip-hop acts. It has become a vital link in the city's live music circuit, and pulls a

regular young and exuberant crowd. Do. 22 De Villiers St, District Six, tel 465 2106, website www.thejam.co.za.

### Kennedy's Restaurant & Cigar Lounge
A lavish all leather and wood venue appointed on Long Street's happening end, dishing up good food and an eclectic jazz line-up Monday to Saturday. Recent performers have included No ID, Blacki and the Brotherhood, and Nadia and Adamu's Latin Afro Combo. 251 Long St, Cape Town, tel 424 1212, e-mail kennedys@netactive.co.za, R10 cover charge for non-diners.

### Maliblues
Maliblues is a slinky upmarket venue serving global cuisine and hosting jazz performers with a smooth, light touch. Jamming sessions are held on Wednesdays, while four-piece bands establish a vibe on Friday and Saturday nights. Upstairs is the Mai Thai Cocktail Lounge, serving Thai cuisine and funky late night groove parties. Closed Sundays. 179 Loop St, tel 422 0393.

### Mama Africa
A colourful, mellow restaurant-bar in the heart of Long Street clubland, Mama Africa features a 12m bar-counter modelled on a green mamba. Marimba and Congolese groups are in the house on a regular basis. The feet start tapping at 8pm every night except Sunday. A popular destination for European and American tourists. 178 Long St, tel 424 8634, e-mail mama@gem.co.za, R10 cover charge.

### On Broadway
Live performances are hosted every night of the week at On Broadway, one of the few venues committed to the city's small but sassy cabaret scene. Drag shows on Sunday and Tuesday, starting at 9pm with a R40 cover charge. 21 Somerset Rd, Green Point, tel 418 8338, e-mail info@broadway.co.za, website www.onbroadway.co.za.

### The Purple Turtle
A cavernous, sleazy bar patrolled by Goths, metalheads and other peculiar creatures of the wee hours. Catch a trio of live bands every Wednesday from about 9.30pm onwards but don't expect elevator music – expect everything from funk to hoghoggetyhog. Cnr Shortmarket & Long St, tel 423 6194, open 11am-late daily.

### Ruby In The Dust
Rickety, sleepy and appealingly decrepit, Ruby's is drenched in subcultural history; for almost twenty years it has been cherished by Cape Town's rasta, punk and hippie communities. Live music, generally reggae or rock, can be heard downstairs, while upstairs there's a peaceful pool bar and a balcony for outdoor herbal pursuits. You'll never find a less uptight venue. 122 Lower Main Rd, Observatory, open 7pm until late nightly.

### West End
Cape Town's premier jazz venue, presenting piping-hot African jazz and fusion performances every week. West End pulsates Thursday through to Saturday night, the rest of the week is more mellow. Contact the club for details of upcoming gigs. Don't dress too casually, and book a good table before arriving if you want to sit down and see the action. College Rd, Rylands, tel 637 9132, e-mail clubgalaxy@iafrica.com, R25 cover charge.

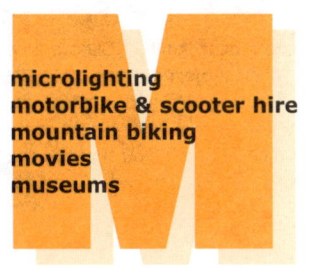

**microlighting**
**motorbike & scooter hire**
**mountain biking**
**movies**
**museums**

# •microlighting

Ever considered taking to the skies in a contraption resembling a cross between shopping trolley and lawnmower. Yes? Then microlighting is for you. It's a thrilling experience offering grand freedom, glorious horizons, and lots of noise. The best inroad to this eccentric mode of aviation is by contacting Aero Sport, the only established microlighting school in the Western Cape, with outlets in Durbanville and Oudtshoorn. They're a friendly bunch, passionate about microlighting and the freedom that follows in its wake. Although Aero Sport's main focus is training aspirant microlight pilots, they'll be all too happy to give you a demo flight. Chances are you'll be addicted in no time. Louis van Wyk, chief flying instructor, will tell you more. Aero Sport, tel 975 3891, cell 083-675 3541, e-mail louisvw@iafrica.com

# •motorbike & scooter hire

Feel like touring the Cape in style and is the spirit of the open road whispering, "four wheels good, two wheels extremely good"? As Robert M.Pirsig and Peter Fonda will attest, travelling by motorcycle mixes senses and soul with the landscape around you. You taste the rushing air, feel the undulating rhythms of the road, and bask in the smiling sun. The Peninsula and the Boland are laced with exceptional biking routes, from epic mountain passes to secret country tracks. If you've got a valid motorcycle license, no bike, and a hankering for adventure, 'tis time to rent a boney and head for the hills.

### African Buzz Scooter Sales & Rentals
The best way to get around the breathtaking Cape Peninsula this summer. No parking or traffic blues, just miles of unadulterated freedom. The Buzz scooters seat two with ease, have electric starters and best of all, no gears. For R160 you get 24 hours of fun, insurance, unlimited mileage, helmet, security lock and a map. Booking's a must! 202 Long St, Cape Town, tel 423 0052, e-mail skootaz@intekom.co.za. 5% discount on all bookings or purchases on presentation of the **Wot to Do Guide**.

### Classic Twin Tours
If the sight of a Harley makes your heart skip a beat, contact Classic Twin Tours about renting one for a day or two. Their majestic range of 1997-model Harley-Davidsons includes Fatboys, Electroglides and Road Kings. Helmets, jackets and unlimited mileage are part of the deal. Expert route advice is given and Classic host riders will happily guide you through the "best big-bike country on earth". Koelenhof, Stellenbosch, tel 882 2558, e-mail enquiries@classictwintours.com.

### Le Cap
Among the bikes available for hire at Le Cap are RGO scooters, 650cc Kawasakis and monstrous 900cc Triumph trailbikes. Most of the bikes are dual-purpose machines, suitable for freeways and backroads. 3 Carisbrook St, Cape Town, tel 423 0823, e-mail lecap@bigfoot.co.za, website www.lecapmotorcyclehire.co.za.

### Mitaka Scooter Rentals
Mitaka rents a wide range of bikes, including funky state-of-the-art scooters, macho cruisers (Harley look-alikes) and chunky on/off road enduros. 345 Main Rd, Sea Point, tel 439 6036, e-mail yaron@mitaka.co.za, website www.mitaka.co.za.

### Thunder Bikes
Rent a shiny Harley-Davidson or a Suzuki Marauder for the day and take to the Cape's highways and byways. Included in Thunder's fee are unlimited mileage, comprehensive insurance, a full tank of gas, open-face helmets and route recommendations. Tel 419 3839, e-mail africatour@icon.co.za, website www.freedomafrica.com.

## •mountain biking

Many of us own mountain bikes, yet few of our fat-tyre friends have tasted the dirt. Odd, because where better than Cape Town to mix mud with bike, body and soul? The city's forests and mountain slopes are loaded with off-road possibility, and although entering some of it is to risk a gauntlet of hikers, hounds, equestrians and khaki-clad officialdom, there are more than enough designated areas that offer both novice and hard-core mountain biker a full course of views and adrenaline.

### Deer Park
Comprising the area below Tafelberg Road, the Park is a web of jeeptracks that provide an informal workout ranging between moderate and strenuous. The gradient is a mixed bag of undulating terrain alternating with steep climbs and sharp descents. With easy access from the city, Deer Park is a great end of day unwinder and in terms of setting alone, one never tires of mother mountain behind and the views of humming city and blue ocean below. Access Deer Park either from Tafelberg Rd or at the top end of Deer Park Drive above Vredehoek. No permit required.

### Tokai Forest
A great introduction if you are new to the dirt, and a favourite haunt among hardened veterans, Tokai is famous for some awesome downhill single track that weaves in and out of the cool setting. The plantation also has an

extensive network of wide dirt roads, and secondary tracks which meander through shady pine, patches of indigenous forest and across small streams. Higher up the slopes of Constantiaberg, pine gives way to rich fynbos and awesome views of mountain and sea. Get there via the M3 towards Muizenberg, exiting at the Retreat/Tokai off-ramp and following Tokai Rd to its end. Tel 712 7471, R8 entry for bikes.

## Silvermine South

Perched high above Noordhoek and False Bay off the Ou Kaapse Weg, Silvermine Nature Reserve is an excellent early morning or late afternoon escape from a week of city humdrum. With the heady scent of fynbos in one's nostrils and a fair degree of physical exertion, the circular 7.2km ride that starts and ends at the picnic spot under pine trees, will work wonders on any flagging spirit. Access from the city is along Ou Kaapse Weg; from the summit continue until the road starts descendng and be prepared for a sudden turnoff to the left. Enter here. No permit needed. Silvermine Nature Reserve, tel 789 2455.

## Jonkershoek Valley

Jonkershoek, just outside Stellenbosch, must rank as one of the most beautiful valleys in southern Africa and is within easy reach of Cape Town for a full morning on the saddle. Framed by a towering wall of rock, punctuated by the Jonkershoek Twins, the valley is a superlative setting of scented fynbos, fern-lined kloofs and spectacular waterfalls. For mountain bikers, Jonkershoek offers a varied off-road experience, including dirt roads, single track and challenging technical sections. Tel 889 1560, open daily, R8 entry.

## Paarl Mountain Nature Reserve

Paarl Mountain Nature Reserve is an impressive landscape dominated by three enormous 500-million-year-old granite rocks. This geological phenomenon offers an unbeatable fish-eye lens view of the Cape Peninsula and Boland mountains and a gradient ideal for several hours of leisurely recreational mountain biking. Cycling is confined to the dirt roads that encircle and bisect the reserve. As the area is open to vehicles you may have to share the tracks with crawling Sunday afternoon traffic, though this should not interfere with your enjoyment. For non-cyclists there are picnic spots and several walks. Tel 872 3658 (weekends).

## Downhill Tours

A good call if you haven't got your own wheels, Downhill Tours lead mountain bike trips down Table Mountain, around Cape Point, and into the Winelands. The beauty of a Downhill tour is that the rides are tailored to the flat, in other words, maximum enjoyment with minimum effort. Tel 422 0388, e-mail downhill@mweb.co.za.

## Rent 'n Ride

A friendly hire shop that, apart from bikes stocks roller-blades, quad bikes and jet-skis. For about R60 a day you can hire an 18-speed Avalanche mountain bike. 1 Park Rd, Mouille Point, tel 434 1122, e-mail bahamab@iafrica.com, open 10am to sunset.

## Want to know more?

*A Guide to Mountain Bike Trails - Western Cape* (Red Press), is aimed at those who have the wheels but don't know where to use them, offering detailed advice on 24 mountain bike spots in the Cape Peninsula and wider Western Cape. All levels of riders are catered for, with trails ranging from 4km to several days in the saddle.

## •movies

Forget jogging, tai-chi and pottery – a big fat juicy flick is the only sure cure for serious boredom. For a two-hour, popcorn-strewn appointment with the Global Celluloid Authority (Hollywood, California), you will be billed between R15 (matinees) and R30 (main evening show), which is no problem if it's a good film. The Mail and Guardian carries the best film review section around – but don't let someone else's opinions cow your instincts.

### Mainstream Theatres
Mainstream Hollywood releases are shown at several commercial cinemas all over town, all of which advertise in the Cape Times and Cape Argus. The most fashionable, with plush seats and Dolby surround sound are the Ster-Kinekor and Nu-Metro theatres found in the city's more trendy malls. Buy your ticket at the door or by phone with Ticketline, tel 918 8960.

### Ster-Kinekor Cinema Nouveau
With an outlet in Cavendish Square (tel 683 4063/4), and the V&A Waterfront (tel 425 8222/3), Cinema Nouveau screens only art-house and foreign-language films. A little pretentious, but the films are often unmissable.

### The Labia
Once the grubby, flea-bitten shrine of alternative cinema in Cape Town, the Labia has been given a welcome revamp in recent times and now offers an intelligent mix of art films, cult classics and new releases on four screens. Friendly staff and tasty and affordable snacks are available. Screenings are advertised in the daily papers, while programmes are distributed at various outlets. 68 Orange St, Gardens, tel 424 5927, e-mail labia@new.co.za, website www.labia.co.za.

### Nedbank Imax Theatre
The screen is huge (15 metres high), the sound is huge, and the pleasure is huge. You won't catch Hollywood actors at the Imax: the stars are jungles, mountains, seas and animals, all brought to you with superb cinematography and thunderous sensory impact. Each documentary is screened for a few months, and all of them are worth catching. Entrance is R34 for adults and R25 for kids and seniors, and screenings are hourly, between 11am and 9pm (10am-10pm in peak season). BMW Pavilion, cnr Portswood & Beach Rd, V&A Waterfront, tel 419 7365, e-mail info@imax.co.za, website www.imax.co.za.

### Independent Armchair Theatre
An innovative club-cum-cinema which screens cult and art movies with a video projector. The only place in town where you can adopt a near-horizontal position on a comfy couch, swig beer and watch a movie, all simultaneously. Screenings on weeknights – contact the venue for details, or collect a programme when in the area. 135 Lower Main Rd, Observatory, tel 447 1514.

# •museums

It has been scientifically proven that the frayed post-millenial human brain responds positively to an afternoon of pottering among curious objects and beautiful old things. So dip your cerebellum into Cape Town's museum circuit, which offers the leisurely prowler everything from stuffed quaggas to priceless Dutch masterpieces to struggle T-shirts and holy rugby boots. For antique freaks, there's also a liberal supply of meticulously preserved historic homes. Entrance charges are very modest by international standards and most museums ask no more than R5 per visitor.

### Bo-Kaap Museum
Built in 1763, the museum house is one of many fine examples of early urban Cape Dutch architecture in the historic Bo-Kaap area. There's a photographic display, a traditional bridal chamber and an abundance of Muslim material culture. An intriguing window into the past, the Bo-Kaap Museum will detain you longer than its size might suggest. 71 Wale St, tel 424 3846.

### Cape Medical Museum
Housed near the Waterfront in the Old City Hospital for contagious diseases, the Cape Medical Museum is a stroll through the antiseptic corridors of the Cape's medical past. Among the displays are turn of the century reconstructions of a consulting room, a dentist's room, an operating theatre and a hospital ward. The museum also contains a traditional medicine display featuring indigenous and healing plants, as well as a collection of unique and scary instruments of medical torture. You'll leave thinking, Thank the Lord for 21st century medical technology! Portswood Rd, Green Point, tel 418 5663, open Tues-Fri 9am-4pm (Sat & Mon by appointment).

### Cape Town Holocaust Centre
A sensitively assembled examination of genocide, the Cape Town Holocaust Centre is a powerful virtual journey into the past. The exhibition combines text, photographs, archival film footage and documents, multi-media displays and recreated environments. South Africa's relationship with the Holocaust is explored, and the testimonies of survivors bring great immediacy to the visitor's experience. A lesson on the tragic consequences of unchecked racial prejudice. 1st floor Albow Centre, 88 Hatfield St, Cape Town, tel 462 5553, e-mail ctholocaust@mweb.co.za, website museums.org.za/ctholocaust, open Sun-Thurs 10am-5pm, Fri 10am-1pm, closed on Saturdays and Jewish holidays, entrance free.

### Castle of Good Hope
As the oldest surviving building in South Africa the Castle is a museum in itself and ranks among the best preserved of its kind built by the Dutch East India Company. A stroll within its pentagonal bastions, across the courtyard and down to the dungeons and prison cells, is an atmospheric glimpse into the past and one well worth taking. Besides home to the Western Cape military command HQ, it houses the famous William Fehr Collection, a superb exhibition of Cape ceramics, metalware, furniture and

art dating from the 17th to 19th centuries, and the Castle Military Museum. The Grand Parade, Cape Town, tel 469 1084, entrance R15 adults, children R6.50, open 9am-4pm daily.

## District Six Museum
Atmospheric, uncluttered and understatedly emotional, the District Six Museum is a sensitive memorial to the legendary inner-city neighbourhood. Much of the floor is covered by a giant street map of District Six as it was before the bulldozers arrived; ex-residents have marked their houses on the map. The museum also features superb photographic exhibits, and the staff are dedicated and keen to answer your questions. 25a Buitenkant St, tel 461 8745, e-mail info@districtsix.co.za, website www.districtsix.co.za, open Mon-Sat 9am-4pm.

## Groot Constantia Manor House & Wine Museum
The original Cape Town wine estate, Groot Constantia was allotted to Simon van der Stel in 1685 and has been home to many a fermenting grape ever since. The Manor House Museum is a classic Cape Dutch affair fitted out in 19th-century style, with a collection of fine furniture and European porcelain. Another attraction is the Wine Museum, where you can pore over wine-consumption gear dating back to 50BC. In summer you can join a tour of the Groot Constantia cellars every hour; in winter there are tours at 11am and 3pm. Groot Constantia Estate, Constantia, tel 794 5067, open 10am-5pm daily.

## Josephine Mill Museum
For a peaceful pit-stop in verdant surroundings, look no further than the Josephine Mill – the city's only functional water-mill. Named after a Swedish Crown Princess in 1844, the Mill continues to make flour on a shady bend of the leafy Liesbeeck River. Your options here include watching a milling demonstration and purchasing the end result, enjoying a meal in the tea garden, or simply strolling and meditating to the river's whisperings. Boundary Rd, Newlands, tel 686 4939, open Mon-Fri 9am-4pm, Sun 10am-4pm, closed Sat.

## Koopmans De Wet House
A genteel 18th century townhouse once owned by the stylish socialite Marie Koopmans De Wet, notable for its murals, blue-and-white VOC porcelain, Delftware, and refined Cape and European furniture. An enclave of old-world charm in the heart of the concrete jungle. 35 Strand St, Cape Town, tel 424 2473, open Tue-Sat 9.30am-4.30pm, entry R3 adults.

## The Mayibuye Archive
Dig into this country's heroic, confusing, terrifying and inspiring recent history at the Mayibuye Archive. Here you can explore a mountainous treasure-trove of artwork, posters, documents, videos and oral history recordings – all relating to apartheid and the difficult job of destroying it. The Archive is more an overflowing library than a user-friendly museum, and you'll need a little initiative to get the best out of it. An invaluable record of the battles of the recent past. Library Level One, University of the Western Cape, tel 959 2954, open 9am-4.30pm, Mon-Fri.

## Michaelis Collection
If you're hanging out on Greenmarket Square and it all becomes too noisy and *deurmekaar*, escape into the Old Town House for a hefty dose of woody old-world gravitas. Once Cape Town's city hall, this elegant building has

been holding court over the Square since 1766, and houses a remarkable collection of paintings by 17th century Dutch and Flemish masters. The Collection also hosts superb visiting exhibitions of graphic art and cartoons. Old Town House, Greenmarket Square, tel 424 6367, open Mon-Fri 10am-5pm, Sat 10am-4pm, closed Sun.

## Natale Labia Museum

Once upon a time a certain Prince Natale and his Princess Ida Labia lived a refined life in a beautiful mansion overlooking the sea… Today the mansion is a museum and cultural meeting-place. The Natale Labia is full of filigreed ceilings, elegant furniture and fine European paintings, and also entertains poetry readings, lectures and concerts, and mounts contemporary art exhibitions. Quality breakfasts and snacks are available at the Café Labia, on the ground floor. 192 Main Rd, Muizenberg, tel 788 4106, e-mail nlm@gem.co.za, website www.museum.org.za/sang, open 10am-5pm, Tues-Sun, entry R3 (Sundays free).

## The Rugby Museum

A temple to the gods of the funny-shaped ball, the Rugby Museum is the nostalgic rugby fan's dream. Scrum down and ruck your way through memorabilia, photos, videos, jerseys and paintings. The emphasis, naturally, is on Springbok and Western Province rugby. Boundary Rd, Newlands, tel 686 2151, open weekdays 9.30am-4pm.

## Rust-en-Vreugd

The building is a dignified 18th century townhouse, and inside it you will find an intriguing range of pictorial art from the William Fehr collection – among the works on display are paintings by the renowned Thomas Baines. Rust-en-Vreugd is an essential stop-off for anyone interested in Cape Town's eccentric colonial past. There's a peaceful garden out back, and contemporary paintings are exhibited upstairs. 78 Buitenkant St, tel 465 3628, e-mail wfehr@iafrica.com, open Mon-Sat 8.30am-4.30pm, entry free (donations welcome).

## South African Jewish Museum

A high-tech visual and interactive experience housed in a landmark building clad in Jerusalem stone, the South African Jewish Museum depicts 150 years of Jewish history in South Africa. The setting is impressive – a hybrid of Cape Town's oldest synagogue with ultra-modern architectural influences – and the story, contextualized within South African history, is poignantly conveyed with impressive multi-media displays, photographs, religious artefacts and installations. 88 Hatfield St, Gardens, tel 465 1546, e-mail viv@sajewishmuseum.co.za, website www.sajewishmuseum.co.za, open Sun-Thur 10am-5pm, Fri 10am-2pm, entry R20 adults, R10 children, R15 senior citizens & students (with ID).

## South African Maritime Museum

The country's largest collection of ship models can be seen at the Maritime Museum, a place which will give goosebumps to those susceptible to the salty romance of the open ocean. The Museum focuses on early seafarers around the SA coast, and the development of Cape Town's harbour, with special displays on the Union Castle Passenger Line, local shipwrecks, and the whaling industry. You can also stomp around aboard a rare World War II boom-defence vessel moored at the Museum. 17 West Quay, Table Bay Harbour, tel 419 2506, e-mail museum@maritimemuseum.co.za, open 10am-4.45pm daily, entry R10.

## South African Cultural History Museum

The building was once a slave lodge and later the Cape Colony's supreme court, and the Museum's collection focuses on the early years of European settlement at the Cape. Among the many artefacts are 17th century "postal stones" – under which passing sailors deposited letters to later visitors. To antique freaks and those interested in the texture of everyday colonial society, the Museum is highly recommended. Others may find it gloomy and tedious. Cnr Adderley & Wale St, tel 461 8280, open Mon-Sat 9.30am-4.30pm, entry R7 adults, R2 children.

## The South African Museum

The biggest and oldest museum in the country, the SA Museum's exhibits span natural history, zoology, archaeology and geology – enough for a full afternoon of bug-eyed perusing. The most dramatic display is the Whale Well, where you can hear the big ol' fish singing their odd tunes while viewing their big ol' skeletons, which are suspended, to spine-tingling effect, from the ceiling. Elsewhere you'll come across stampedes of glassy-eyed stuffed animals, a wealth of indigenous cultural artefacts, and a controversial and fascinating Bushman diorama. The Museum's a prime destination for kids, as well as adults who still enjoy feeling gobsmacked. 25 Queen Victoria St, tel 424 3330, open daily 10am-5pm, entry R8 adults, children no charge (all free on Wednesdays).

## SA Naval Museum

Housed in a Royal Navy mast-house built in 1815, this museum documents the history of the South African Navy and its imperial predecessors. Photographs, paintings and historical articles are spiced up with uniforms, swords and other cool nautical stuff. The Museum also boasts mock-ups of two submarine compartments, the bridge of a minesweeper and a genuine air-raid shelter. The Mast House, West Dockyard, Simon's Town, tel 787 4635, e-mail thekidz@mweb.co.za, open 10am-4pm daily, closed Christmas Day, New Years' Day and Good Friday, entrance free.

## Simon's Town Museum

A lot has gone down in Simon's Town over the centuries, and the subject matter in the Museum extends from the early activities of the Dutch East India Company to the 19th century heyday of the Royal Navy to the eviction of 7000 residents under the Group Areas Act in 1967. The building is the Governor's Residence, dating back to 1777: the original slave quarters have been preserved. Court Rd, Simon's Town, tel 786 3046, e-mail stmuseum@mweb.co.za, open Mon-Fri 9am-4pm, Sat 10am-4pm, Sun 11am-4pm, entrance by donation.

## Telkom Exploratorium

Want to play a gigantic electronic foot piano? Want to make your voice sound weird? Then get yourself down to the Telkom Exploratorium, a snappily-designed museum focusing on Light, Sound and Electricity. There are enough cool gadgets and gimmicks here to keep your brain bleeping and fizzing for some time. Union Castle Building, V&A Waterfront, tel 419 5957, open Tues-Sun 9am-6pm, entry R10 adults, R5 kids.

## Warrior Toy Museum

Vintage toys of every description can be admired at the Warrior Toy Museum, from dolls and dinky toys to meccano sets, model cars, boats, trains, planes and soldiers. This is a small paradise if you're very short in the tooth, and pleasantly nostalgia-inducing if you're not. St George's St, Simon's Town, tel 786 1395.

**nature reserves
nightlife: clubs
bars**

# •nature reserves

Part of the magic of the Cape Peninsula is that, no matter how crowded the city, one is always a stone's throw from the countryside. Not only are we one of few cities with a nature reserve right on the doorstep, but it's a richly flavoured liquorice-all-sorts nature reserve. Sea, mountain and forest, they're all here in abundance, and each is home to a unique universe of plants, animals and insect life that is yours to enjoy virtually free. Included in this fragile splendour is the mountain chain that extends from Lion's Head and Signal Hill all the way south to Cape Point. The variety of plant life found between both ends is staggering – 2285 species at last count, two-thirds more than the British Isles combined! So get out there and hug a tree today.

### Silvermine

Silvermine Nature Reserve is the high-lying section of the peninsula mountains extending from Muizenberg in the east to Noordhoek in the west. Access is from Ou Kaapse Weg (M64) which more or less bisects the reserve. With lots of mountain greenery, this is a favourite weekend haunt for braai enthusiasts (fires allowed in the northern section only), botanists, hikers, mountain bikers and scenery seekers. There's something for them all. Entrance to the reserve is near the summit of Ou Kaapse Weg. Tel 789 2455, open 8am-6pm summer, 8am-5pm winter, R5 entrance fee (& R10 per vehicle).

### Cape of Good Hope Nature Reserve

The Cape of Good Hope Nature Reserve, or Cape Point as it is locally known, is a place of cliffs and sea and blustery winds that is right up there among the sights that most foreign visitors are here to see. A funicular railway takes you from the carpark to the lookout point, but you really get the feel of the place only by doing it on foot. Eroded cliffs are pounded by waves rolling in all the way from South America, and the phantom hulk of the Flying Dutchman is out there for eternity. It's definitely a moody place, with lots of rugged scenery. Detour to a few of the beaches to appreciate it fully – like Buffelsbaai, Bordjiesdrif and Maclear, or take a long and lonely walk past the wreck of the Thomas T Tucker at Olifantsbos. Several hiking trails put you out in the fynbos among the eland, bontebok, rhebok and Cape mountain zebra. Tel 780 9010, e-mail capepnt@concor.co.za, website www.capepoint.co.za, open daily, 7am-5pm winter, 7am-6pm summer, entry R20 adults, R5 children.

## Kirstenbosch Botanical Garden
Kirstenbosch is another childhood memory of a refuge from the ordinary and a place where you were allowed to run and roll on the grass. The real interest is not just the botanical aspect, which is overwhelming if you consider not just the plants themselves, but the academic and environmental aspects. It's also Kirstenbosch's layout and situation, and the opportunities it presents for walks and hikes. Springtime is most colourful but there's always something bursting into flower. Breakfast at a choice of three restaurants makes a fine start to an unambitious day. 70 Rhodes Drive, Newlands, tel 799 8899, website www.nbi.co.za, open throughout the year, 8am-6pm winter, 8am-7pm summer, entrance fee R15 adults, R5 children.

## Rondevlei Nature Reserve
Rondevlei is a pool of the tears that were cried by a princess who lived in the cave called Elephant's Eye on Constantiaberg, hundreds of years ago. Today, it's a great place for bird-watching, with towers, hides and a trail – and some hippo that were reintroduced to the lake about 20 years ago. Access is off Victoria Rd into Fisherman's Walk Rd, Grassy Park. Tel 706 2404, e-mail rondevlei@sybaweb.co.za, open daily, 8am-5pm (longer in December), R5 entrance fee.

## Tygerberg Nature Reserve
Tygerberg Nature Reserve has no tigers: the blotchy growth of renosterbos reminded settlers of leopards, which they unaccountably called tigers – a case of too much Klippies and Coke we thinks. What Tygerberg does have is a magical viewsite on the Uitkyk Walk that yields a genuinely panoramic view of greater Cape Town – Table Mountain, international airport and all. An unusual and rewarding reserve for those who think of this part of Cape Town only in terms of Voortrekker Road. Tel 913 5695, open daily (times vary), no entry fee, phone office for directions.

## Helderberg Nature Reserve
Helderberg Nature Reserve is a favourite leg-stretch for the people of Somerset West, but Cape Town is close enough by the N2. Helderberg is a spur of the Hottentots Holland range, jutting out towards the sea, although the reserve is more than this. Spring is a good time for enjoying the pink watsonias massed on the hillsides, but the views are there all year round. There's almost always something happening in the fynbos, which shelters several buck species, caracal, honey badger and even the occasional leopard. Tel 851 6982, open daily 7am-8pm, entry R4 adults & R4 a vehicle.

## Two Oceans Aquarium
Granted, the Two Oceans Aquarium at the Waterfront may be an obviously artificial creation rather than a natural feature, but where else are you going to get a close-up view of life under the ocean, short of taking your clothes off. Delve into the great mysteries of the big blue and experience amazement at the sheer diversity of shape, colour and form. A touch tank and a kelp forest are among the highlights, as are the great whites cruising past like mafia hitmen from the deep. Dock Rd, V&A Waterfront, tel 418 3823, e-mail aquarium@aquarium.co.za, open daily 9.30am-6pm, entry R35 adults, children 4-17 years R18, students/pensioners R28. (See also page 6)

# •nightlife : clubs & bars

A few years ago Cape Town's night scene was a trifle dozy compared to the pulsating party energy of Jo'burg and other fully fledged Big Cities of our planet. But lately things have started to heat up. The new Cape Town is bigger, richer and infused with a constant flow of nocturnal foreigners who add a certain spice to the city's after-dark culture. Nightspots can be divided into two often-blurred categories – on the one hand, a myriad of cafes, bars and live music venues (see Live Music, page 49), and on the other a fluctuating population of out-and-out dance clubs. Night clubs (**C**) tend to live fast and die mysteriously. Also, the best regular parties often hop from venue to venue. Some of the more enduring clubs are listed below, but it's advisable to collect flyers and watch the press for up-to-date info. Topping the charts at most venues is electronic music in all its forms and while mainstream house is numero uno there are strong followings for drum and bass, trance, hip hop, kwaito and latin grooves.

More intimate than The Nightclub but more decadent than The Restaurant (**R**), the 21st century Bar (**B**) is where the ancient and dissolute spirit of Dionysos meets the random communion of the airport departure hall. If you need to seek out sympathetic human company, seduce a stranger, shoot the breeze or just get quietly trashed, Cape Town offers a large lucky-packet of drinking establishments. There are dim, pungent hotel bars, eccentric bohemian dives, hip minimalist cafes, cavernous pool halls and franchised cod-Irish pubs. Take your pick.

## •CITY BOWL

Most of central Cape Town's nocturnal amusements are to be found along a spine of leisure that stretches from Kloof Street in Gardens down Long and Loop Streets and ending around Waterkant Street. Clubs, bars and bistros abound. Occasionally venues are separated by dark and lonely blocks, so if you're up for a club crawl it's best to crawl by car unless you're in a large group. Elsewhere in the City Bowl, De Villiers Street in District Six is a busy and promising party zone.

### 169 on Long (B/R/C)
Long-standing civilized haunt on upper Long Street featuring a restaurant, cool balcony, regular jazz nights and occasional Mo Funk parties. 169 Long St, Cape Town, tel 426 1107.

### All Bar None (B/R)
A fairly recent arrival on famous Greenmarket Square, All Bar None is a place to spot and be spotted in. Two bars, a small dance floor and continental style pavement café make for a multi-purpose hangout in the heart of the city. 26 Shortmarket St, Cape Town, tel 424 9337, open Mon-Sat 11am-4am.

### All Nations Club (B/C)
All Nations adds a welcome splash of roots and dancehall reggae to the city's clubbing spectrum: visit this agreeable spot on Thursday and Saturday nights to skank your Babylon blues into submission. Fridays are dedicated to a fruity blend of world music, hip hop and R&B. The menu is in the Carribean tradition, while the crowd is multi-ethnic and positive. Cnr Buiten & Loop St, tel 083-361 4593, open Thur-Sat, 9pm-late.

### Cohibar (B/C)
A funky split-level venue which features pulsating house and hip-hop parties on weekends. Space on the smallish dancefloor is sometimes in short supply: arrive early or very late if you want to extend your limbs. Popular among a mixed, leftfield student crowd. Longkloof Studios, Darters Rd, Gardens, tel 423 4444.

### Club Georgia (C)
Lively over-25s club that features music from across the African continent, including kwassa-kwassa, kwaito, ndombolo, rai, kizamba and makossa. 30 Georgia St (off Buitensingel), tel 422 0261, open Tue-Sat 9.30pm till very late.

### Club Unity (C)
For unadulterated, high-octane hard house, dance and trance applied to your soul in the company of many happy rhythm slaves, look no further than Club Unity. It's one of the city's premier mainstream dance clubs, offering huge dancefloors, user-friendly chill booths, a cinema lounge, VIP room and 35 kilowatt turbo sound. Shake your ass in luxury. 11 Buitensingel St, tel 424 1248, e-mail clubunity@yahoo.com, website www.clubunity.za.net.

### The Coffee Lounge (B/C)
A low-key, leftfield venue, the Coffee Lounge occupies four storeys and resounds with drum & bass, easy listening, psychedelic trance and funk. The bottom floor is designed for relaxed ambient interaction, all-out dancefloor grooves can be sampled on level four, and other sonic entertainments hover in between. 76 Church St, Cape Town, tel 424 6784, website www.coffeelounge.co.za, open Tue-Sat, 8pm till late.

### The Fez (C)
Stylish venue decorated with Bedouin desert caravans in mind. The DJs are high-profile and keep to the deep and funky end of house for the benefit of a good-looking crowd. An important stop-off on the city's swanky-jol circuit. 38 Hout St, Cape Town, tel 423 1456, open Tue-Sat in season, Wed-Sat out of season.

### Getafix (C)
The neon-and-incense-filled home of the psychedelic at heart. The vibe is deeply untroubled, the soundtrack is unflinching trance. Flail your limbs about and trip out in the company of travellers and hairy marginal people. Chill-out spot by day. 3rd Floor, Unity House, cnr Long & Longmarket St, Cape Town.

### Gijima (C)
Housed in a cavernous building that was once home to legendary clubs like Scratch and The Base, Gijima is a prime venue for languorous deep house and uproarious kwaito. The main dancefloor can be a bit too big and over-lit – make your way to the back room where a kickass vibe develops after 2am. 88 Shortmarket St, Cape Town.

### Groove Central (B/R)
Set to become a hot spot among Cape Town's ritzier set, Groove Central is all leather, dark wood, brass fittings and golden columns. Enhancing the indulgent experience is a long bar, state of the art music system and tasty snack menu. The groovy music features Motown, R&B and occasional live jazz. 72 Barrack St, Cape Town, tel 461 9988.

### The Jam/206 (C)
Two forward-looking clubs that occasionally blend into one, The Jam and 206 are renowned for fat undergound hip-hop parties, electrifying drum & bass evenings and adventurous live music. Come here for an unselfconscious open ambience and space to skank freely. 43 De Villiers St, District Six, tel 465 2106, website www.thejam.co.za.

### The Jet Lounge (C)
A favourite haunt of the beautiful and languid. Up-tempo funky and Latin house are the preferred sounds. Absorb the night air on the balcony overlooking the seedier end of Long Street. Tel 424 8831, 74 Long St (above Blue Moon Café).

### Jo'burg (B)
Top name, top decor, and a top-ranking space in which to loaf and schmooze to a funky downtempo soundtrack. Jo'burg the bar is smaller than the nation's capital and far better-looking. The crowd is diverse with an art-and-media mainstay. DJs on Thursday and occasionally live music on Sunday nights. 218 Long St, tel 422 0142, open 5pm-4am.

### The Lounge (B)
The Lounge has been a long-standing refuge for talented layabouts and new media creatures, and has recently been adopted by a youthful drum & bass set. Boasts a beautiful Victorian balcony overlooking Long Street clubland – bag a table if you can. Jungle, electro and deep house are the staple sounds. Look out for the exquisitely insane light-fittings. 194 Long St, tel 424 7636, open 8pm-2am, closed Sundays.

### Moomba Club Sociale (C)
Among Cape Town's swisher new venues, Moomba hosts deck-ripping parties on Friday and Saturday, while chilled-out Latin tunes are the Wednesday staple. On Thursdays ladies gain free entry and alcoholic potato juice until midnight. 77 Hout St, Cape Town, tel 083-456 2909, website www.moomba.co.za, doors open 9pm.

### More (C)
A meticulously designed venue which aims to satisfy glossy young sophisticates. Lots of plush cubicles, lots of warm colour, and lots of sensual deep house sounds in your ear. More is a nightclub which takes the task of being a nightclub very seriously – and why the hell not? 74 Loop St, Cape Town, tel 422 0544, open Wed, Fri, Sat & Sun, 10pm-late.

### The Piano Lounge (C)
A relaxed, unpretentious house club which attracts one of the most racially-mixed crowds in the city bowl. Drum & bass DJ's do the jump-up thing on Sunday nights. Cnr Loop & Wale St, Cape Town.

### Rhodes House (C)
A late night venue adjacent to the Company Gardens, spread across several lounge and bar areas and an open-air atrium tailormade for a sultry summer night. Theme parties are a stock favourite at Rhodes House, powered by fast beats of a trance, house and rave flavour. Queen Victoria St, Cape Town.

### Rhythm Divine (C)
A popular and airy venue with a solid history of big and eclectic parties. House, funk, hip hop and disco are all on the aural menu. Rhythm Divine features two big dancefloors, a pool room and a mixed, up-for-it crowd. 156 Long St, Cape Town, tel 423 0333, open Wed, Fri & Sat.

### •ATLANTIC SEABOARD
Sea Point has lost much of the glamorous urban vibe it once exuded, but it's still an energetic beachfront 'hood with exceptional sunset views and eateries aplenty. Somerset Road in Green Point, with its parade of gay and gay-friendly bars and clubs, never fails to buzz on weekend nights. The Camps Bay-Clifton strip offers a sprinkling of smart cafes full of sunkissed people, but other than cocktails is fairly limited as a late night stomping-ground.

### 55 (C)
A young and sassy club/bistro attracting a cosmopolitan crowd. The decor can be described as 'warehouse chic', and regular live entertainment includes drag shows and revues (cover charge). 55 takes on its club persona on Fridays and Saturdays (no cover charge). The club's motto is: no heavy attitude from staff, no karaoke and no filthy toilets. 22 Somerset Rd, Green Point, open noon till late.

### BAD - The Bronx, Angels, Detour (C)
A trio of clubs which share a courtyard and a reputation as the nerve centre of Cape Town's gay nightlife. Angels and Detour are two roomy dance venues (R&B and hard house respectively) with a shared cover charge of R40. Bronx is a hugely popular and vibey bar where you can rotate your ass to commercial house, cheesy and Latino grooves. The crowd here is motley, unpretentious and dedicated to the pursuit of a seriously good time. Cnr Somerset & Napier St, Green Point, tel 419 9216 (Bronx), 419 8547 (Angels, Detour), Bronx open nightly, Angels & Detour Fri-Sat.

### Baraza (B)
Baraza" means "meeting-place" in Swahili, and this East-African themed cocktail bar enjoys an outrageous sunset view and a blissed-out equatorial ambience. Catch up-and-coming funk/house DJ's on sultry summer nights. The Promenade, Victoria Rd, Camps Bay, tel 438 1758, open noon till late daily.

### Buena Vista Social Café (B/R)
A small make-believe Cuba overlooking happening Green Point, the Buena Vista Social Café is a relaxed and sociable tapas/cigar bar washed by sultry Latino sounds. The decor is simple – rustic wooden chairs and tables, prints of traditional and Castro's Cuba hanging from the walls, a comfortable balcony with soft cushioned couches. Downstairs you'll find the pumping News Café and swish Belgium restaurant Zero932. 1st Floor Exhibition Building, 81 Main Rd, Green Point, tel 433 0611, open daily from 4.30pm.

### La Med Bar & Restaurant (B/R)
Paragliders stop off at La Med after their dizzying descent from Lion's Head to the sports field next door. Overlooking the rocks at Clifton, La Med is an

evergreen sundowners venue for the jovial and debauched. The sunset view is phenomenal, even from ground level. Glen Country Club, Victoria Rd, Clifton, tel 438 5600, e-mail lamed@kristensen.co.za, website www.lamed.co.za, open daily.

## •V&A WATERFRONT

The V&A Waterfront has much to offer if you feel like eating well and your budget is loosely packed. At the end of the day, however, it's a massive mall, and you're unlikely to find anything here that approaches an authentically hedonist atmosphere.

### Den Anker Restaurant & Bar (B/R)

A busy and boisterous pub haunted by tourists and well-heeled locals. Belgian beers are Den Anker's speciality, both on tap and in a bottle. One of the more spirited venues in the Waterfront, but a touch too vacuum-packed to take seriously. V&A Pierhead, tel 419 0249, e-mail denanker@mweb.co.za, open 11am-12pm daily.

### Ferryman's Tavern (B/R)

A congenial pub near the Waterfront's main entrance, Ferryman's has 12 varieties of draught beer, a huge sunny beer garden, tasty pub meals, and an air-conditioned restaurant upstairs. Frequented by a smartish thirtysomething crowd. East Pier Rd, Waterfront, tel 419 7748, e-mail ferrymans@mweb.co.za.

### Quay 4 Restaurant & Tavern (B/R)

A big and busy pub overlooking the water at the heart of the Waterfront, Quay 4 offers a cheerful outdoors vibe, good seafood pub meals, and live cover bands nightly at 9pm. A sedate sit-down meal can be had in the restaurant, while downstairs the tavern is favoured by a boisterous rugby-and-ale crowd. A wide range of bottled and draught beers are available. Quay 4, Victoria Basin, Waterfront, tel 419 2008.

## •CAPE FLATS

The Cape Flats offers tremendous party opportunities, but there is no compact nightlife neighbourhood and good venues are scattered across a wide area. For a safe and groovy "shebeen crawl" through Guguletu, Langa and Mandalay contact Township Music Tours, tel 426 4260, cell 082-921 1126.

### Club Galaxy (C)

A straight-up dance club playing R&B and mainstream house, Galaxy caters mainly to a youthful coloured crowd. But it's also a legendary *jolplek* of years gone by: on some evenings the crowd indulges in old-*skool* "jazzing" – the quintessential Cape Flats dance move. College Rd, Rylands, tel 637 9132, open Thu, Fri, Sat, 8pm till late (Sat from 3pm), e-mail clubgalaxy@iafrica.com.

### Club Images (C)

A big flashy venue featuring a karaoke bar, a sports bar and a spacious dancefloor. Live jazz on Thursday nights, while DJ's follow the spirit of the crowd on Fridays and Saturdays. R&B and mainstream house are the sonic bread and butter. Claude St, Athlone Industria.

### Club Vibe (C)

If you are suffering from an intense desire to shake your booty, pay a visit to Club Vibe, a sprawling superclub patronised by a swanky coloured crowd. Two dance-floors (mainstream and uplifting house), 100 television screens, and a revolutionary sound technology feature known as "The Earthquake" are some of Club Vibe's drawcards. Friday nights are young with muchos beats per minute; Saturdays see a more sedate crowd annexing the dance floor. Cnr Rigel & Castor Rd, Lansdowne, tel 762 8962, e-mail clubvibe@club-vibe.com, open Fri & Sat from 9pm.

## •Northern Suburbs

Until a year or two back there wasn't much happening on the far side of the boerewors curtain, but this is gradually changing as the green grid-locked suburbs are snapped up by well-heeled twentysomethings in search of a nightlife alternative to SABC.

### Dockside (B/C/R)

This is perhaps the biggest and swankiest nightspot ever to sprout from Capetown soil. Dockside is a palatial megaclub, incorporating a hi-tech dance arena, a rainforest-themed cocktail bar, a dedicated jazz venue, a restaurant, a Belgian beer cafe, and an exclusive rooftop bar called Monte Carlo's. This is a good venue for huge events with big-name DJ's, but it's all a bit excessive if you're after a simple, authentic jol. Century City (exit Sable Rd, N1), tel 552 2030.

## •OBSERVATORY & WOODSTOCK

Once a deeply stoned village inhabited by odd people in which nothing much went on, Observatory is now a deeply stoned village inhabited by odd people in which quite a lot goes on. The legendary leftfield suburb has sprouted a busy pleasure district in and around Lower Main Road, liberally stocked with bars, restaurants, wacky shops and internet cafes. A large floating population of backpackers and immigrants has adopted Obs, and her shabby-but-pretty old streets vibrate with a young and footloose energy. It's a safe and compact area to wander through until the wee hours. Nearby Upper Woodstock promises to become a useful leisure zone, with a handful of quality venues on Roodebloem Rd.

### 89 on Roodebloem (B)

89 is a minor triumph of elegant, low-key design, housed in a vintage Victorian cottage. In winter there's a soul-warming hearthfire, and all year round there's a welcoming and intimate ambience. 89 can prove very addictive. 89 Roodebloem Rd, Woodstock, tel 447 0982, open 6pm-1am, closed Sun & Mon.

### The Curve Bar (B/C)

A slick industrial style venue in what used to be the old Bijou bughouse. The ex-Magnet guys entertain here with a selection of classic cocktails and a Latin Jazz-Ambient blend of music. Live bands and DJs are a regular feature over weekends. 178 Lower Main Rd, Observatory, tel 448 0183, cell 082-689 8288, e-mail trebok@mweb.co.za, open Wed-Sat 8pm until late.

### Don Pedro's (B/R)

Don Pedro's has been a source of good cheap food and scruffy charm since the eighties, when it was the chosen rendezvous for struggle activists. The kind of place where you can drink and talk for hours without sensing moral pressure from the waitrons. 113 Roodebloem Rd, Woodstock, tel 447 4493, e-mail info@donpedro.co.za, website www.donpedro.co.za, open daily 9am until late.

### Café Ganesh (B/R)
Café Ganesh is Observatory's rootsy heartbeat. It's the natural habitat of a crazy salad of marginal types: artists, writers, performers and BA students. They brew the coffee with admirable patience, the felafels are morish and the decor is – to attempt a definition – comical third world chic. If it's crowded, a spontaneous kwaito party may erupt. 66 Lower Main Rd, Observatory (cnr Trill Rd), tel 448 3435, open 6pm daily, closed during July.

## •SOUTHERN SUBURBS
If truth be told, nightlife in the lands south of Observatory is a tad dull. Drowsy locals can be found in most neighbourhoods, and there is a string of instant Irish pub-in-a-can establishments catering to their needs. But there ain't a lot else nearing the authentic thing.

### Barristers Grill & Café on Main (B/R)
For years a landmark among the pub set, Barristers has recently shed its image as an all dark-wood hideaway for male beer drinkers and carnivores to one encompassing a fairly cosmopolitan bar and restaurant, popular among the local BMW set. Cnr Kildare Rd & Main St, Newlands, tel 674 1792, open daily.

### Blink (C)
A popular new club in Claremont catering to mainstream partygoers. 80 Main Rd, Claremont, tel 671 5535, doors open 9pm Mon, Wed, Fri & Sat.

### Café Sirens (C)
A busy club catering to a preppy suburban crowd, Café Sirens features live jazz on Tuesday nights and comedy acts on Wednesdays. Commercial hits and classic rewinds move the floor on weekends. Dress code smart casual, with the emphasis on "smart": sneakers are considered tacky. 80 Main Rd, Claremont.

### Foresters' Arms (B/R)
Deep in the leafy interior of Newlands you'll find "Forries", a venerable home-from-home to sporty students and grey-suited professionals. A woody and unassuming pub in the Anglo-Celtic tradition, it boasts a tree-lined courtyard for pleasurable day-time drinking. Grab a bench and dwell on England. 52 Newlands Ave, Newlands, tel 689 5949, open Mon-Sat, 10am-11pm, Sun 9am-4pm.

### Kuzma's (B/R)
A down-loose student hangout that seems to have been around for ever. Kuzma's serves tolerable Greek(ish) food and hosts a motley and talkative tribe of drinkers deep into the night. By far the most animated venue in prim Rondebosch, and it stays open round the clock – in fact, the doors haven't shut for six years. 91 Main Rd, Rondebosch, tel 689 3762.

### Springfield 2 (C)
Rave kids, goth kids and drinking kids escape to Springfield 2, a sprawling club on Newlands railway station. Divided into alternative rock, house and pop floors, Springfield is loud, debauched and just a little bit weird. Sport Pienaar Rd, Newlands.

### Taboo (C)
A lonely but determined outpost of dance music in the depths of the southern suburbs, Taboo teems with cleancut students and underage suburban kids interacting to a 80's and 90's house/techno mix and other dance anthems of the day. Cnr Main Rd & Roscommon Rd, Claremont, tel 683 5651.

## •FALSE BAY & BEYOND

A few miles from the slick nightspots of Cape Town's city centre, False Bay seaboard boogies along in a world of its own. Nightlife along the drag from Muizenberg to Simon's Town and further is a down to earth cultural soup of surfers, middle-aged hippies, wannabe artists and working-class school kids. The attraction is often less the venue than the ocean setting.

### The Brass Bell (B/R)

Neatly squeezed between the sea and the railway line, The Brass Bell is a superb weekend hangout open from noon to late. Munch on *slap* chips and calamari (four restaurants available), peer at the purple mountains across the bay, and dunk yourself in the tidal pool when the urge hits you. Pure bliss, especially when a live band is belting out your favourite tunes. The Station, Main Rd, Kalk Bay, tel 788 5456, open from noon daily.

### The Red Herring (B/R)

The Red Herring boasts an open-air deck called Skebangas, overlooking the panoramic Noordhoek valley. A fine watering hole when wandering down the peninsula, that's usually packed with clean-cut twenty-somethings out to natter and quaff cider in the sun. Cnr Pine & Beach Rd, Noordhoek, tel 789 1783, e-mail theredherring@iafrica.com, pub open Mon 5pm, Tues-Sun 11am-12pm (restaurant shorter hours).

**paragliding
penguins
picnics
planetariums
poetry readings
pool bars
putt-putt**

## •paragliding

Inventors, visionaries and lunatics have been strapping themselves to winged contraptions and leaping off mountains for centuries – often with unhappy consequences. But many hard lessons have been learnt, and unpowered flight is now an advanced science, with paragliders across the globe soaring and circling in perfect silence, with the regal grace of eagles. If you envy the city's floating population but feel you don't have the time, guts or money to join them, consider a shortcut to the skies: take a tandem flight with an experienced pilot. Flights range between 15 minutes to 45 minutes. Prices are consistent, and the usual routine is to buy a flight voucher in advance, and fly when the weather is suitable. The most popular locations are Lion's Head, Signal Hill, Sir Lowry's Pass, Porterville and Hermanus. No experience and no feathers required.

### Paraglide Cape Town

Attach yourself to experienced paraglider Ian Willis and explore the meaning of freedom. R450 buys you a ticket to the skies of either Clifton, Hermanus, Sir Lowry's Pass or Franschhoek (in winter). All equipment is provided as is a good measure of encouragement. Also on offer from Paraglide Cape Town is a comprehensive introductory course to the sport. Tel 082-727 6584, e-mail ian@hi-xposure.co.za, website www.hi-xposure.co.za/pgct.

**Parapente**
For an instant ticket to the sky, strap your body to a qualified Parapente instructor and on 3-2-1, take a leap into the unknown. The experience has little parallel and is potentially addictive. For the latter group Parapente offers a course – 1 x paraglider, harness, stuff bag, packpack and helmet are provided, together with expert tuition on how to be a bird. Tel 762 2441, e-mail wallenda@iafrica.com.

# •penguins

Cape Town's penguins won global fame during their sensational life-and-death struggle with a villainous oil slick in Table Bay. Most of the African penguins were safely evacuated to Port Elizabeth while the slick dispersed – and like many other Capetonians abroad, the birds swam briskly home without delay. You can spend quality time with these winning waddlers at Boulders Beach south of Simon's Town (tel 786 2329, entry R10 adults, R5 kids), where they lead gormless, carefree lives among the rocks and pools. They have no fear of people, but don't hassle them. Most of the Cape's penguins live on Robben Island and other smaller islands – turn to Boat Cruises (page 21) for a chance to see these island ecosystems from the water. There are also penguins lodging at the World of Birds (tel 790 2730), SANCOB (tel 557 6155) and at the Two Oceans Aquarium (tel 418 3823) where you can see them in their favoured element – underwater. No more Mister clumsy bird.

# •picnics

Ingredients for a fine day out: one times wicker basket, check cloth, straw hat, hamper of deli best and fine bottle chilled white. Capetonians are slowly warming to the idea that you don't need to spend a fortune on bad service and substandard food to enjoy a meal out. Among conservative and trendy, macho and dandy, the picnic has finally gained a universal thumbs-up. And, with the invention of ciabatta and basil pesto, gone are the days of your common garden picnic and with it tea the taste of tin and government loaf. Go the solo route with your own picnic or treat yourself with the ready-made item. Either way, a picnic on the beach, under a forest canopy or out in the country is a sure-fire means of having a good and relaxing time.

## Beaches
Camps Bay, Clifton One, Two, Three and Four are Cape Town's favourite picnic beaches. Get there as the sun takes a dip into the horizon and you'll find peppered across the sand, small gatherings of laid-back citizens quaffing wine and munching on snacks ranging from McBeal-inspired to lavish culinary creations.

## Boschendal
Boschendal seeps with history – gabled Cape Dutch buildings framed by majestic mountains, towering oaks trees and manicured gardens. Absorb this richness by way of the Boschendal al fresco Pique Nique, served under fragrant pine trees. On offer for about R65 a head, are hampers filled with terrines, salads, cold meat and cheese. Booking is essential. Tel 870 4274.

## Buitenverwachting
A world removed in the heart of Constantia, Buitenverwachting is a serene wine estate of gracious gabled buildings, beautifully manicured gardens and territorial ducks. The estate offers a luxury picnic hamper for about R60 a throw, filled with fancy cheese, paté, chicken roulade, salmon mousse and home-baked bread. Wash it down with a bottle of fine estate wine under historic oaks and the experience will be a truly memorable one. Klein Constantia Rd, Constantia, tel 794 2122, cell 082-973 8543, picnics available Mon-Sat 12.30pm-2.30pm, booking necessary.

## Kirstenbosch National Botanical Garden
For a picnic in a gorgeous and secure setting Kirstenbosch can't be beat. Acres of rolling green lawn fringed with flowers and ancient shady trees yield numerous spots to spread out a blanket and spend a full afternoon munching on Woolies wonders, reading the Sunday Times and eyeballing a steady procession of camera-laden tourists dressed in khaki. 70 Rhodes Drive, Newlands, tel 799 8899, website www.nbi.co.za, open throughout the year, 8am-6pm winter, 8am-7pm summer, entrance fee R15 adults, R5 kids.

## Newlands Forest
Gentle walks under shady pine, gushing streams and twittering birdlife make Newlands Forest a prime picnic zone. The official site is within earshot of Rhodes Drive but on weekends there are enough kids and car stereos to muffle the traffic noise. For an altogether more serene experience head a little deeper into the forest and enjoy an hour or two far removed from life as you know it. Get there via the M3 above Newlands. Newlands Forestry Station, tel 689 7438/9.

## Silvermine Nature Reserve
A beautiful and popular spot at the top of Ou Kaapse Weg, Silvermine has picnic and braai spots, fynbos, fine views and gentle strolls. Summer weekends tend to be crowded and the reserve is susceptible to the vagaries of the Cape Doctor. Access is near the summit of Ou Kaapse Weg. Tel 789 2455, open 8am-6pm summer, 8am-5pm winter, R5 entrance fee (& R10 per vehicle).

## Spier Wine Estate
As is the case with most local wine estates you can't take your own food along to this heavily visited weekend destination. Instead you'll find the Farmstall Deli, stocked with a range of delectable picnic goodies. Select your favourite items or opt for a ready-made hamper, then seek a shady spot near the ornamental lake to munch it. A little too popular in summer. Off Baden-Powell Drive, en route to Stellenbosch (N2), tel 809 1159, open daily 9am-5pm (6pm in season).

**Tokai Forest**
A serene forest filled with exotic trees from across the globe, Tokai harbours more than enough shady nooks and crannies for a prostrate afternoon chewing on tasty things and good thoughts. Close by is a thatched tea room and ablution facilities. A sensible choice if the south-easter is up and blowing. Tel 712 7471, entry free.

## •planetariums

Ever questioned your place in the universe? Or just seeking a moment out from earth reality? Part of the South African Museum complex, the green-domed Planetarium offers a guided virtual safari into the wonders of the cosmos. Visitors recline in an arena of dentist's couches and gawk into space as multiple projectors recreate the night sky over several light years – past, present and future. If you've ever looked at the stars and wished you knew something about them, a trip to the Planetarium is essential. But, be prepared for sudden and giddy thoughts about your earthly insignificance. 25 Queen Victoria St, tel 424 3330, showtimes Mon-Fri 1pm, Sat & Sun 12pm, 1pm, 2.30pm, Sat & Sun children's shows 12pm, entrance adults R8, children R5.

**SA Astronomical Observatory**
For more star-gazing, visitors to the SA Astronomical Observatory in Obs are treated to a tour and an opportunity to press eyeball to lens and gaze upon the stellar landscape. The observatory houses the historical McClean refractor, the largest telescope in the Western Cape. If the weather's bad you'll have to settle for a slide or video show. Phone 447 0025 for the details. Observatory Rd, Observatory (between River Club and Valkenberg Hospital, open every second Saturday of the month (all visits must be booked in advance).

## •poetry readings

Many dismiss the art of poetry as self-indulgent and a waste of time. Not that poets and poetry-lovers care much about this, since they're too busy splashing about in secret and thrilling pools of human truth that can only be accessed through the inspired arrangement of nice words. So there! While Cape Town is home to volumes of talented poets, their shyness and/or anarchism prevents them from airing their rhymes as often as they should. But a couple of venues have ignited the flame of spoken poetry and you can help keep it burning. Also watch the press for once-off readings and book launches.

### Dorpstraat Café

Students, academics and Stellenbosch mavericks gather at the Dorpstraat Café on the first Monday night of each month to swap poetic explosions and meditations. The sessions begin with readings by four or five established poets – and then the floor is opened to rookie wordsmiths. Most of the poetry is in Afrikaans, but English contributions are welcome. 59 Dorp St, Stellenbosch, tel 886 6107.

### Chilli 'n Lime

On Tuesday nights at around 8pm, Chilli 'n Lime hosts a popular evening entitled "U4Ever", which besides being a lot of fun serves as a platform for upwardly mobile artists and others hoping for a brief moment of glory. The watchword is dynamic free expression, with poetic performances interspersed with live music. 23 Somerset Rd, Green Point, tel 419 3648, cell 083-590 8157 (organiser), e-mail u4ever001@hotmail.com, R20 entry.

## •pool bars

One of America's greatest contributions to modern civilisation, pool is a noble and cultivated game. Well, not really. It's a trashy and mindless game, but it offers cheap and sociable entertainment and improves your hand-eye co-ordination. Some people experience periods of heightened Zen awareness in a noisy pool hall – an effect created by the glow of green felt, the savour of cold beer, an evergreen hit on the jukebox, and the mystically agreeable feeling of knowing, as you line up a tricky shot on the black, that it will trickle obediently into the corner pocket. Cape Town has a handful of large pool halls, and many bars and clubs have a solitary table lurking in their innards.

### Stones (Observatory)

A gigantic pool bar with more tables than you could shake a stick at, Stones is always teeming with fresher kids and grizzled pool freaks. The music is a very odd blend of seventies biker rock and teeny hits. Even odder is the management's insistence on "no headgear" – if someone earnestly asks you to remove your hat, they ain't mad and they ain't kidding. On balmy evenings, be sure to cool your boots on the superb balcony overlooking vibrant Lower Main Rd. Cues and tables rating: 7/10. 94 Lower Main Rd, Observatory, tel 448 9461, open 12pm till late.

### Stones (Cape Town)

A replica of Observatory's Stones in the city centre. Same decor, same fish tank, same number of tables and same music policy – but the vibe and the clientele are somewhat seedier. Boasts a well-appointed balcony overlooking Long Street that's good for an afternoon beer or two. Cues and tables rating: 7/10. 166a Long St, tel 424 0418, open noon until late.

### The Shack
An always-busy student favourite, the Shack is equipped with five tables and a good supply of excellent fine-tipped cues – with these babies a ludicrously ambitious cut shot becomes a feasible option. Other fillips are a huge window providing city views and fresh air, and agreeably varied music. Stays lively deep into the wee hours. Cues and tables rating: 8/10. 45b De Villiers St, District Six, tel 461 5892.

### The River Club
A large portion of this gigantic building is devoted to the pool gods. The crowd ranges from seedy afternoon drinkers to networking suits attracted by the Club's golf-driving range. A bit short on personality, but The River Club is a decent place to have a game or two if you're in the area. Tasty meals are available from the adjacent restaurant, and major sports matches are shown on big screens. Cues and tables rating: 7/10. Observatory Rd, Observatory, tel 448 6117.

## putt-putt

You can't network with company execs on a putt-putt course, but in almost every other respect putt-putt is a superior pastime to golf. It's far cheaper (at R8.50 per player for 18 holes), and far quicker. You don't have to walk up and down endlessly looking for your balls, and you don't need special shoes or underwear. There are eighteen holes in a putt-putt course: you've got a good shot at a hole-in-one on the first, but as you progress you will grapple with increasingly outlandish and treacherous obstacles. Putters, balls, scorecards and pencils are provided: all you need are hands, eyes and a stout heart.

### Beach Road, Three Anchor Bay
Many golf courses are famous for their fine settings. The putt-putt course in Three Anchor Bay is no exception – crashing ocean and a view of Robben Island across the marine drag. Trash the opposition on one of two courses and celebrate with a cappuccino at the friendly Newport Market and Deli, found a little way down the road. Three Anchor Bay, tel 434 6805, open 9.30am-9pm.

### Beach Rd, Muizenberg
Two courses, both par 2 but one more challenging, are on offer at this putt-putt venue backdropped by the Indian Ocean and distant False Bay mountains. Tel 788 8800, open 9am-9pm (10pm in summer), R8.50 a round.

### Putt-Putt Enterprise, Durbanville
An 18-hole course located in the cavernous Tyger Valley Centre. Putt-putt Enterprise is a good place for a quick round before or after a heavy bout of shopping. Tel 914 2008, open Mon-Fri 10am-10.30pm, Sat-Sun 9am-11pm, entry R8.50.

**quad biking**

## •quad biking

The quad bike can be described as a funky, chunky hybrid of a go-kart, a scrambler and a miniature tractor. This novel and slightly insane off-road vehicle has four fat wheels, plenty of fire in its belly and much to offer if you fancy exploring the mad, bad and ridiculous approach to driving. Quad biking is easy, safe and pretty exhilarating… let your inner minibus taxi-driver emerge in a rustic environment.

**Cape Quad Trails**
Cape Quad Trails lets you burn rubber on terrain including sand and bush, climbs, descents, "technical sections" and flat-out straights. Muddy river crossings are an option for the adventurous, while alternative routes are provided for more timid quadders. Available for group and corporate outings. Melkbos 4x4 park, R27 (West Coast Road), tel 083-321 6990, e-mail stepup@mweb.co.za.

ratanga junction
record & CD shops
restaurants
rhodes memorial
robben island
rock-climbing
roller-blading

## •ratanga junction

Once upon a time in Cape Town, an outlandish metropolis of cycads, plastic monsters and artificial waterfalls sprouted mysteriously near the N1 freeway. Some locals believed it was a hotel for extraterrestrial sex tourists, while others claimed it was the head office of a bizarre cult started by Sol Kerzner and Homer Simpson. Finally it emerged that the strange structure was an amusement park called Ratanga Junction, and it's been amusing the masses ever since with an array of impressive rides. Ratanga's flagship attraction is The Cobra, a gutwrenching roller-coaster that hurls you around in vast lunatic loops at 100km/h. If you're perversely unwilling to experience deep and unnecessary terror, shun The Cobra – and perhaps call a raincheck on the Congo Queen, a giant swinging ship which pushes the frontiers of nausea-inducing technology. Slightly less brutal but nonetheless stimulating are the two excellent watery rides, Crocodile Gorge and Monkey Falls. In the Hippo Hollow you'll find fun rides for kids of all ages. Ratanga Junction also boasts a giant screen cinema, live entertainment in the evenings, and a range of restaurants. It's well worth a visit. Sable Road exit off N1, toll-free tel 0861 200 300, e-mail info@monex.co.za, website www.ratanga.co.za, open Wed-Sun 10am-5pm.

## •record & CD shops

Shopping for music is a deeply pleasurable activity and one of the sanest ways to blow your shekels ever invented. While CD prices at the ubiquitous Musica chainstores are, on the whole, marginally lower than at smaller outlets, service can be scruffy. By contrast, independent stores are obliged to compete for your buck with efficient ordering, good advice and general agreeableness. Bargains aplenty can be found at second-hand CD stalls on most street markets. Seek and ye shall hear.

### The African Music Store
A small, funky and friendly store specialising in popular sounds emanating from this continent. The emphasis is on quality ahead of quantity: you won't find every available African record here, but you'll find the very finest in hi-life, Afro-jazz, kwassa-kwassa and plenty more. 90a Long Street, tel 426 0857.

### Look & Listen
Look & Listen (ex-Max Megastore) is a sprawling palace of music in the heart of a glittering retail Babylon, with enough CDs to boggle the mind and obliterate the bank balance. The range is impressive, with very comprehensive jazz, classical and African sections. Videos, DVDs, accessories and computer games will also try to come home with you. The listening facilities generously permit you to hear the whole of each track. 1st floor, Cavendish Square, Claremont, tel 683 1810.

### Outlaw Records
A popular second-hand record chain, Outlaw Records carries an eclectic if erratic collection of music, ranging from boere-country to gangsta rap. As with all second-hand shopping, luck and effort are the secret here; you'll find cut-rate gems if you prowl the shelves systematically. Bring along unwanted CDs and LPs – they may be translatable into cash. Outlets on 55 Castle St, Cape Town, tel 423 8145; Maynard Rd, Wynberg, tel 797 2482; and 45 Main Rd, Claremont, tel 671 7887.

### Rugged Vinyl
Frequented by DJ's and amateur beat freaks, Rugged Vinyl stocks a diverse

range of imported vinyl, with the emphasis being on drum & bass, breakbeat and progressive house. If you fancy a spot of mixing and scratching yourself, you can also buy turntables, needles and record bags. 158 Long St, tel 424 1248.

### Sessions Music World
An outpost of Musica, Sessions is the only record store in town devoted almost entirely to classical music and jazz, and stocks everything from Gustav Mahler to Vanessa Mae. Ground floor, Victoria Wharf Centre, V&A Waterfront, tel 419 7892.

### Syndicate Records
The Syndicate is a vibey store catering mainly to the vinyl requirements of house DJ's, but it also stocks a good range of dance CD's and a selection of club gear and accessories. A favourite daytime stopover for gelled-and-platformed club kids. Mutual Building, Parliament St, tel 465 2532.

# •restaurants

Gone are the days when eating out in Cape Town was a grand occasion limited to a main course of steak, steak or steak. The city is now a cosmopolitan mixed grill – Thai, Californian, African, traditional Cape Malay, pseudo Italian, seafood in various guises, fusion ("international contemporary"), and a long chain of Americanisms – vie side by side for your tastebuds. With the advent of Café Society, the emphasis has also shifted from starchy service and gruelling culinary epics to relaxed eateries where atmosphere is as important as the food itself.

Although you'll find restaurants across the city, the art of fine and less fine dining tends to be concentrated in specific pockets. Sea Point's Main Road was for long the hub of the local restaurant scene but its image has become a little tattered over the years. A long rash of restaurants still dominates the main drag but the fickle market has shifted its gaze elsewhere. Much of this move has been up the road to Green Point and the Waterfront, a virtual food (and clothing) emporium.

With 50 or so restaurants, the Waterfront's menu reads long and covers everything from Creole, Chinese, continental, Italian, Portuguese and sushi to the ubiquitous Spur burger. Prices tend to be higher at the Waterfront than elsewhere, service can be erratic over high season, and few of the restaurants show much in the way of traditional character. On the plus side, there is free parking, tight security and a wide selection of venues – a winning combination as far as tourists and most locals are concerned.

For a more adventurous experience, the long spine running from the high end of Long Street through to upper Kloof Street has spawned a rash of restaurants, many trying awfully hard to be original and cosmopolitan and serving everything from noodles to nachos to north Indian curry. The atmosphere along this spine is altogether more alive, prices are a bit lower than the Waterfront and many of the restaurants display individual style. Freelance parking attendants, street kids and limited parking is the downside.

Heading to the sea, Camps Bay and the False Bay strip between Kalk Bay and Simon's Town have pockets of restaurants, some excellent, others characterful, and still others a pleasing combination of both.

Beyond these concentrated culinary zones you will find, buried in shopping malls and suburban neighbourhoods, further eateries, a few gourmet notables among them but on the whole nothing to write home about.

This all said, here then a handpicked basket of recommended local restaurants suited to different hours, budgets and palates.

## •BEST BREAKFAST, BRUNCH & LUNCH

A windless weekend, shimmering ocean to the front and mother mountain to the back, what more quintessentially Cape Town than kicking back, indulging the tastebuds and watching the world pass slowly by? The current preference among breakfast, brunch and lunch devotees is for light meals, fresh ingredients and good coffee. And, as important as the food itself, is the setting: if it ain't cooking it probably ain't worth it.

### Alphen Hotel
A leafy context of historic buildings and shady oak trees. The Boer and Brit pub is a convivial refuge offering good old English alehouse atmosphere, a hearty menu and massive log fires in winter, while outside you'll find a relaxed terrace to while away the weekend hours. Alphen Hotel, Alphen Drive, Constantia, tel 794 5011, open 9am-12pm.

### Barnyard Farmstall
Down to earth family venue in country setting, featuring chickens, rabbits, a rusty old tractor and plenty of wholesome food like grandma used to make. Try the breakfast – it's tailormade for a sumo wrestler. Steenberg Rd, Tokai, tel 712 6934, open daily for breakfast, lunch and afternoon tea.

### The Brass Bell Restaurant
A Cape institution squeezed between Main Rd, railway line and Indian Ocean, famous for sundowners, live music, reasonable food, and a generally fab time. The Brass Bell has four eateries and a menu of seafood, Asian and pizzas; alternatively, head for the terrace and down a boerewors roll with a pint of your favourite ale. The Station, Main Rd, Kalk Bay, tel 788 5456, open lunch, dinner daily.

### Café Adagio
Under milkwood trees and next door to the well-known Red Herring, Adagio is a sedate spot to celebrate a long walk on Noordhoek Beach. The English breakfast will quell the most stubborn hunger but the rest of the menu is light day fare. Cnr Beach & Pine Rd, Noordhoek, tel 789 1320, open daily 9am-5pm.

## Café Mozart
A long-time resident on happening Church Street, Mozart's a perfect Saturday morning stop-off between shopping and browsing the antique markets and art galleries. The breakfast and lunch menu is varied and the final tab pleasingly low. 37 Church St, Cape Town, tel 424 3774, open Mon-Fri 7am-3pm, Sat 8am-1pm.

## Café Whatever
A friendly place with an unhurried Obs personality serving foamy, fragrant and fresh Arabica espresso roast coffee and quality light meals. Also a useful low-key pit-stop before or after a night on the town. 90 Lower Main Rd, Observatory, tel 448 9129, open daily 11am-2am.

## Carluccis
Among a handful of neighbourhood cafés, Carluccis perches away from the humdrum in upper Oranjezicht. Freshly ground coffee and solid open sandwiches tend to dominate the plates of loyal patrons. A second outlet has recently opened its doors to the Bantry Bay jet-set. 22 Upper Orange St, Oranjezicht, tel 465 0795; 29 Victoria Rd, Bantry Bay, tel 439 6476, open 8am-8pm.

## Company Gardens Restaurant
Buried under a rush of beautiful trees and exotic plants, and serenaded by pigeons and other feathered species, this outdoor eatery in the Company Gardens has for long been a soothing weekend refuge for battle-weary locals. The restaurant is managed by the Provincial authorities and the menu tends to reflect the tight budget – nothing particularly special but good value nevertheless. Open daily.

## The Daily Deli
A tiny French-style café in upper Tamboerskloof, the Daily Deli is particularly quaint, with a sunny view of Lion's Head, great coffee and a get-to-know-thy-neighbour sociability. 13 Brownlow Rd, Tamboerskloof, tel 426 0250, open 8am-10pm daily.

## Gallery Café
Housed in the SA National Gallery, this elegant café is open for breakfast, lunch and tea, with a menu featuring sandwiches, salads and pasta. A serene pitstop between browsing museums and the Company Gardens. South African National Gallery, Government Avenue, tel 465 1628, open Tues-Sun 10am-5pm.

## Giovanni's Deliworld
Trendy hangout with Italian temperamento and far too few chairs. Excellent coffee and a wide range of tasty deli items are available – sip on a cappuccino, close the eyes and think of Sicily. Main Rd, Green Point, tel 434 6893, open Mon-Sat 8.30am-9pm.

## Groot Constantia
Choose between a cheery pub-style eatery or the traditional Jonkershuis Restaurant at this historic wine estate. The Jonkershuis dishes up wholesome food, from Malay curries to bredies and seafood, served in the courtyard or indoors. Groot Constantia Rd, Constantia, tel 794 6255, open daily for breakfast & lunch, dinner Tue-Sun.

## Kirstenbosch National Botanical Garden
On offer at this national landmark are three new restaurants – a small coffee shop, a self-service diner and a formal sitdown. All are fine, but none

quite capture the quaint spirit of Kirstenbosch's old eatery (since closed), where roast beef, mashed potatoes and apple pie was a Sunday ritual for many. Rhodes Avenue, Newlands, tel 799 8899, open daily 8am-7pm (6pm in winter).

## Le Petit Paris
For a number of years, a place to see and be seen, on Greenmarket Square. Coffee and croissant at Le Petit Paris is best timed for Saturday morning when ex-models, local celebs and other wannabes emerge from the woodwork. 36 Burg St, open Mon-Sat.

## Melissas
Kloof Street Melissas is the flagship, with two others – in Newlands and Constantia Village – following in its wake. The place is invariably packed out for breakfast and the expensive buffet lunch. A tantalising assortment of pastries is on hand for Canderel-and-carrot cake housewives. 94 Kloof St, Tamboerskloof, tel 424 5540, open daily, 7.30am-8pm, 8am-8pm weekends.

## Newport Market & Deli
What was once a tacky corner café is now a friendly deli and coffee shop serving a towering café au lait and other tasty treats. Nestle up to a frothy cappuccino and gaze upon a distant Robben Island and Mouille Point's passing parade of nubile rollerbladers... 47 Beach Rd, Mouille Point, tel 439 1538, open daily 8am-8pm.

## New York Bagels & Sitdown Deli
A novel concept featuring a labyrinth of food stations, manned by unsmiling but efficient teams of staff, dishing up everything from high cholestrol breakfasts to stirfries, burgers and a thousand bagel permutations. Over weekends the place buzzes, with brunch and lunch leaning towards the frenetic. 51 Regent Rd, Sea Point, tel 439 7523, open daily till late.

## Noordhoek Farm Village
A sprawling barnyard of tie-and-dye craft shops and three outdoor eateries set under oaks near the start of Chapman's Peak. Frazzled parents can enjoy their chocolate cake in peace while the offspring do their thing in the adjacent playpark. Noordhoek Farm Village, Noordhoek (just off Chapman's Peak Drive), tel 789 1317, open daily 8.30am-5pm (later in season).

## Old Cape Bistro
Sitting alongside the Old Cape Farmstall, this is a pleasant venue slumbering under massive oak trees, good for breakfast, lunch and afternoon tea. Erratic service and prices pitched at tourists tend to be the downside. Groot Constantia Rd, Constantia, tel 794 7062, open daily 8.30am-5pm.

## Olympia Café & Deli
Kalk Bay's rustic answer to Melissas, a high-turnover eatery brewing up a weekend storm of fine coffee, massive omelettes (about 12000 a year!), pastries and freshly squeezed juice. It's an extremely popular spot so expect to wait for a table. 134 Main Rd, Kalk Bay, tel 788 6396, open daily for breakfast, lunch and light meals, Thu-Sat for dinner, closed Mon.

## Peddlars on the Bend
A regular hangout among the Southern Suburb set, with tables in an enclosed garden and a raucous indoor pub and English-style restaurant attached. The fare is pricey but solid. Spaanschemat River Rd, Constantia, tel 794 7747, open for lunch & dinner daily.

### Penguin Point Café
An understated restaurant about 48 steps from the Boulders' penguins – reasonably priced food and an ocean view are the other lures. Breakfast is served from 7.30am, with a choice of full English and a simple but good-value continental buffet. 4 Boulders Place, Simon's Town, tel 786 1758, open daily 7.30am-10pm.

### Primi Piatti
Invariably packed with slick and shiny Atlantic Seaboard residents, Primi Piatti offers cheeky and zippy service, sea views and heaped portions dominated by pasta, pizza and salad. Sibling outlets can be found on Greenmarket Square (Primi's flagship and recommended), the V&A Waterfront, Constantia and Canal Walk. 18-21 Victoria Rd, Camps Bay, tel 438 2923, open Tues-Sun breakfast, lunch and dinner.

### The Red Herring
A firm Cape Town favourite offering a relaxed open-air deck with pub and ocean view and a comfortable restaurant with a blazing winter fireplace. Good for a lazy summer or wintry lunch or dinner. Cnr Beach & Pine Rd, Noordhoek, tel 789 1783, restaurant open Tues-Sun 12am-3pm, 7pm-10pm.

### Rhodes Memorial Restaurant
A soothing thatch-and-stone outdoor venue with a grand appointment above the city and a wide-ranging menu of home-cooked fare. Whether for breakfast, lunch or Sunday tea with grandma, Rhodes Mem is recommended though the recent price hike is likely to chase the locals away. Rhodes Memorial, Rondebosch, tel 689 9151, open daily 9am-5pm.

### The Village Café
An awfully quaint sidewalk café in the heart of Waterkant's gay neighbourhood. Sipping on an espresso, gazing upon the harbour through a cobbled alley of old buildings, one could well be seated in downtown San Francisco. Considering the café's postage-stamp size, the menu is impressive – a range of good value breakfasts, daily specials and all-time favourites, among them Cape Malay mince, chicken schnitzel and Sunday roast. 159 Waterkant St, De Waterkant, tel 421 0632, open daily from 7.30am (closing times vary).

## • BEST AFTERNOON TEA
The Queen's drink is as popular as it ever was on this sunny foot of Africa and a number of establishments, many located in gorgeous leafy or coastal settings, are dedicated to brewing the perfect cuppa.

### Josephine Mill
A sedate spot resting under oaks near Fedsure Park cricket grounds (ex-Newlands Stadium), that's good for a snack and Sunday tea. In summer, Sunday jazz sessions inject some life into the old lady. Boundary Rd, Newlands, tel 686 4939, open Mon-Fri 9am-4pm, Sun 10am-4pm, closed Sat.

### The Gardeners Cottage
Another soothing escape in the shade of ancient pine trees, the Gardeners Cottage is a sure bet for early afternoon tea with gran or latest romantic conquest, as it is for breakfast and lunch. 31 Newlands Ave, Newlands, tel 689 3158, open Tues-Fri 8am-4.30pm, Sat-Sun 8.30am-4.30pm, closed Mon.

### Mount Nelson Hotel
The Pink Nelly may appear daunting to the pocket but for an indulgent high tea in a truly grand setting amidst beautiful gardens, it can't be beat. On offer is an all you can eat buffet tea, held every day between 2.30pm-5.30pm – you may even bump into the Queen's mother herself! 76 Orange St, Gardens, tel 483 1000.

### Radisson Hotel
Gorgeous outlook a foghorn blast from the Waterfront, the Radisson (ex-Villa Via) is also fast becoming famous for an all-you-can-stuff buffet tea. A relaxed and stylish spot to while away the afternoon hours. Beach Rd, Granger Bay, tel 418 5729, open for tea and cake daily, 12.30pm-5pm.

### Vineyard Hotel
Only a block away, yet far removed from the madness of Claremont's CBD, the Vineyard's beautiful garden with a view of Devils Peak, is an elegant and calming venue tailored to a fine cup of Ceylon or a late afternoon G&T. Anything more might blow your budget. Colinton Rd, Newlands, tel 683 1520, open daily.

## •BEST SUNDOWNERS
Food and drink tastes even better as the sun fades slowly to orange, red, before dissolving into the horizon. For this perfect combination get your bod to the following spots.

### Baraza
An island-style wine bar with a hip twenty-something clientele, overlooking the Camps Bay main drag. The cocktail menu is extensive, the cane chairs are comfortable, the music is loud and the bodies are beautiful. The Promenade, Victoria Rd, Camps Bay, tel 438 1758, open noon till late.

### Blues
Window seats are at a premium but the vista of humanity below and the shimmering ocean across is worth shuffling in queue for. Enjoy anything from a beer to a cocktail, to bubbly with Knysna oysters. The Promenade, Victoria Rd, Camps Bay, tel 438 2040/1, open lunch and dinner daily.

### Café Paradiso
An eternal favourite among locals and tourists alike, Paradiso offers outdoor seating on benches, a view of Table Mountain and a substantial menu. Relaxed spot for a late afternoon snack and drink, followed possibly by dinner inside. 110 Kloof St, Tamboerskloof, tel 423 8653, open daily 9.30am-11pm.

### Caprice
Deli-cum-restaurant set downwind from the main Camps Bay beachfront throng, with a long list of cocktails and wide, albeit pricey, menu and buffet. 37 Victoria Rd, Camps Bay, tel 438 8315, open breakfast, lunch and dinner daily.

### Cool Runnings
New kid on the Kloof Street block (opposite Café Paradiso), Cool Runnings is a Jamaican Island concept – or at least, someone's interpretation of a Jamaican Island – that promises to be a summer hotspot on the sundowners circuit. 108 Kloof St, tel 424 8388, open 9am until late.

### Doodles
Located right on the beach in the heart of Table View, this is one of Cape Town's oldest cocktail bars with a strong line-up of shooters and other lethal concoctions. A sheltered bamboo deck ensures that your drink stays on the table and the sand out of your mouth. 110 Beach Boulevard, Table View, tel 554 1331, open 9am-12pm.

### Dunes
A social hub on Hout Bay's beachfront known for a relaxed atmosphere. The attached playground will keep the kids distracted while you suck on a stiff cocktail. Beach Rd, Hout Bay, tel 790 1876, open 9am-10.30pm.

### La Med Restaurant & Bar
An Atlantic institution between Camps Bay and Clifton, famous for an amazing ocean outlook and hangovers from hell. Glen Country Club, Victoria Rd, Clifton, tel 438 5600, open 12pm-9pm (bar later).

### La Playa
Probably the only coffee shop at the V&A Waterfront that faces the setting sun, good for cappuccino and pre-movie sundowners. V&A Waterfront, tel 418 2800, open daily 9am until late.

### The Sandbar
Trendy beachfront spot in Camps Bay, ideal for cocktails and light meals, nachos and towering salads among the latter. 31 Victoria Rd, Camps Bay, tel 438 8336, open daily 10am-10pm.

### Table Mountain Bistro
For spectacular sunsets you won't get much better than the top of Table Mountain. Head up by cablecar, quaff a memorable sundowner, follow it perhaps with dinner, and hitch a ride with the last car down. Tel 424 0015, open 8am-9.30pm.

## •BEST DINNER SPOTS
Going out for dinner is good for the soul and a deadcert way of blowing hard-earned cash. You needn't fork out a fortune to enjoy a good meal out, at the same time eating on the cheap doesn't necessarily pay either. This said, the following is a selection of Cape Town's surer evening bets, all with a reputation for good food, consistent service and pleasant ambience, with options priced between low ($), moderate ($$) and high ($$$), and suited to different occasions and tastebuds.

### Africa Café ($$)
Though a tad less authentic than in days gone by, the Africa Café is still probably your best bet for a broad range of African cuisine. On the table are dishes from across the continent – for about R80 a head you can join the tourists and try most. Heritage Square, Shortmarket St, Cape Town, tel 422 0221, open daily for dinner.

### Au Jardin ($$$)
The lush Newlands garden and mountain views are idyllic and the French menu is unlikely to disappoint – one would hope so given the prices! Ideal venue for an intimate or special occasion. Vineyard Hotel, Colinton Rd, Newlands, tel 683 1520, open lunch Tue-Fri, dinner Mon-Sat.

### Bacinis ($)
Found way up Kloof Street, away from the bustle, Bacini's is a homely venue draped in flags and other sentimental soccer memorabilia. Besides a pleasant vibe, the menu is a wholesome one, dominated by pastas and carefully-assembled pizzas. Limited outdoor seating is also available. 177 Kloof St, Gardens, tel 423 6668, kitchen open 10am-10.30pm.

### Barristers Grill & Café on Main ($$)
Many southern Suburbers will swear that this pubby Newlands landmark serves the best steaks in town. Non-carnivores will find more contemporary fare in the sociable adjacent café. Cnr Kildare Rd & Main St, Newlands, tel 674 1792, open Mon-Sat for breakfast, lunch and dinner, Sun from 5pm.

### Beluga ($$$)
You're likely to bump into one or other high profile local at Beluga – a cavernous restaurant housed in an old foundry. Attached is a plush cocktail bar, lounge and café (open 10am until late), spilling onto a pleasant courtyard lined with designer shops. Beluga's menu is an innovative fusion of classic and contemporary cuisine – by no means inexpensive but always packed with well-heeled thirty-somethings. The Foundry, Prestwich St, Greenpoint, tel 418 2948, restaurant open lunch Mon-Sat, dinner daily.

### Bloemers Kosteater ($$)
"Lekker boerekos" is the cuisine and over the top Afrikaner kitsch is the decor. Oxtail, *hoenderpastei*, *bobotie* and marrow bones are a taste of what you can expect – all fairly priced and generously heaped onto the plate. Weekends at Bloemers feature a pianist. 85 Roodebloem Rd, Woodstock, tel 448 0256, open lunch Tue-Fri, dinner Mon-Sat.

### Blue Danube ($$$)
Owned and managed by an affable Swiss couple and set in a Victorian house in Tamboerskloof, the Blue Danube is relaxed, the service personal without being overbearing, and the food an innovative Euro-African fusion – as in, crepinettes of springbok, roast rump of Karoo lamb with rocket purée and pecorina cakes... 102 New Church St, Tamboerskloof, tel 423 3624, open dinner Mon-Sat, lunch Tue-Fri.

### Bukhara ($$$)
A cavernous eatery with the acoustics and regular crowd to match, Bukhara is arguably the best and certainly the most popular curry den in town. The menu, featuring north Indian classics, is sweetly spiced and the flavour of each item is subtly distinct from the next. 33 Church St, Cape Town, tel 424 0000, open lunch Mon-Sat, dinner Mon-Sun.

### Cape Colony ($$$)
Want to impress your date and have the credit card for the job? The Mount Nelson is the way to go. The setting is a throwback to a grand hotel of the colonial past: faux animal prints, colonial palms, a Victorian Table Mountain mural... The menu however, is firmly rooted in the present, featuring snoek, crocodile, springbok and samoosas. 76 Orange St, Mount Nelson Hotel, Gardens, tel 483 1000, dinner daily.

### Caffé Balducci ($$)
An in-the-mall café-restaurant that started out a tad overly self-conscious. With age however, this Waterfront venue has become a lot more relaxed and a good place to meet up for drinks, a meal and an opportunity to ogle toned bodies. Victoria Wharf, V&A Waterfront, tel 421 6002/3, open breakfast, lunch and dinner daily.

### Café Bardeli ($$)
Flagship of several similar-styled trendy bar-cum-deli restaurants in the city, Café Bardeli dishes up good deli fare till late, gorgeous bodies and a groovy soundtrack. Its siblings, Long Street Café and Obz Café are pitched much along the same lines. Longkloof Studios, Darters Rd (off Kloof St), Cape Town, tel 423 4444, open daily 8.30am till late (kitchen closes 11pm).

### Café Dharma ($$)
A slick Indonesian-styled joint of cane and big cushioned couches split between humming courtyard bar and indoor restaurant serving a fairly expensive mix of novel and more recognisable dishes. The clientele is a yuppie twenty-something dressed in black. Get with it! 68 Kloof St, Gardens, tel 422 0909, open for dinner and drinks daily.

### The Cellars-Hohenort ($$$)
It will set you back an arm and a leg but the Cellars Restaurant, ranked among planet earth's top 50 eateries by readers of Condé Nast magazine (if that means anything!), is well worth the splurge. The verdant Constantia setting is gorgeous and the general presentation and service is impeccable. Couples are ensured an intimate candlelit experience, while groups can book a private dining room with own patio, in what used to be the cellars. 93 Brommersvlei Rd, Constantia, tel 794 2137, lunch and dinner daily.

### Chai Yo ($)
It may be located in a drab Mowbray neighbourhood but Chai Yo is unpretentious and invariably full. The service is fairly efficient and the Thai-dominated menu tasty and well priced. 65 Durban Rd, Mowbray, tel 689 6156/7, open daily for lunch and dinner.

### The Codfather ($$$)
A good seafood restaurant leaning towards the expensive, offering a rotating sushi bar – where morsels of the raw delicacy are delivered to you by way of conveyor belt – and a main sitdown section with 12 types of fish to choose from. The best seats are at the window but there aren't many of them. 41 The Drive, Camps Bay, tel 438 0782, open lunch and dinner daily.

### De Goewerneur ($$$)
Join Van Riebeek for dinner at the historic Castle of Good Hope, a civilized experience best reserved for a special occasion. Dining takes place in one of several private rooms adorned with original artworks by the likes of Pippa Skotnes and John Kramer, and the traditional menu is in keeping with the rich historical theme. Good venue for an intimate dinner with a small group of friends. Castle of Good Hope, Buitenkant St, Cape Town, Tel 461 4895, open lunch & dinner Tue-Sat, Sunday lunch.

### Dias Tavern ($)
A no-frills institution near the Taxman's office that dishes up a twice-daily storm of killer Portuguese food and authentic atmosphere. Don't be daunted by the subway-like entrance and motley decor – great things happen in the kitchen. The Portuguese cuisine is the tastiest and probably the best value you'll find in Cape Town. 27 Caledon St, Cape Town, tel 465 7547, open for lunch & dinner Mon-Sat, booking advisable on Friday.

### Diva ($)
A busy and convivial Italian-themed eatery in Observatory, Diva offers fairly snappy service, palatable prices and some pretty fine pizza. 88 Lower Main Rd, Observatory, tel 448 0282.

### Don Pedro's ($)
A late night institution that's been around as long as the city itself – or so it seems. Don Pedro's a favourite haunt among insomniacs and, since its general revamp, a progressively more yuppie clientele. A laid-back spot offering good value and friendly service. 113 Roodebloem Rd, Woodstock, tel 447 4493, open 8am until around 3am.

### Emily's Bistro ($$$)
A campish venue – blue walls, zebra stripes, melodramatic art works – in upper Woodstock, with an exciting and innovative menu that breathes fresh life into South African cuisine: "Wilde Willemien", "Patataland" and "Tswana Love Call" are among the dishes you can expect! 7 Roodebloem Rd, Woodstock, tel 448 2366, open Mon-Sat.

### The Famous Butchers Grill ($$)
It lies buried in a nondescript hotel, but the Famous Butchers Grill is talk of the town among local carnivores. The steaks come in a handy range of Mrs, Mr or Meneer sizes and a variety of coatings. Carnivore heaven, or what?! Days Inn, 101 Buitengracht St, Cape Town, tel 422 0880, open for lunch Mon-Fri, dinner Mon-Sat.

### Fishmonger Hout Bay ($$)
An Ocean Basket concept in the sleepy hollow of Hout Bay, serving fresh seafood in a pan, affordable prices and uncomplicated atmosphere. Chalked up daily on the board, along with the hake and calamari standards are several exotic linefish prepared in different permutations. Winter sees a huge fire blazing inside, while in summer the crowds gather under the milkwood tree. 33 Victoria Rd, Hout Bay, tel 790 7760, open Tue-Sun for lunch & dinner.

### Five Flies Restaurant & Bars ($$)
Waiter, waiter, what the heck are these flies doing in my soup?! Housed in a national monument, Five Flies is an elegant yet contemporary space comprising several interleading rooms, each stylish as the next, and two plush bars. The menu changes periodically and is well-priced for a relaxed yet memorable night of indulgent gastronomy. 14-16 Keerom St, Cape Town, tel 424 4442, open lunch Mon-Fri, dinner Mon-Sat.

### Floris Smit Huijs ($$)
Created and owned for several years by local restaurant aficionado Etienne Bonthuys, the Floris Smit Huijs has passed through several hands since, but is still a vibrant venue with eclectic decor and a menu influenced by north Africa, the Mediterranean, the East, and would you believe it, South Africa. 55 Church St, Cape Town, tel 423 3414, open lunch and dinner daily.

### Fujiyama ($$)
The decor is break-away avant-garde but the menu is firmly rooted in Japan. The result is an interesting hybrid that pegs Fujiyama among the city's better sushi haunts. 100 Main Rd, Sea Point, tel 434 6885, open lunch Mon-Fri, dinner daily.

### Happy Wok ($)
China, Vietnam, Indonesia and Japan feature side by side at this inexpensive and no-hassle eatery on Kloof Street. The portions aren't huge but you'll come away satisfied. Good for a pop-in pop-out meal. 62 Kloof St, Gardens, tel 424 2423, open daily for lunch and dinner.

### Hatfields ($$)
Cosy ambience, consistent service and a solid middle-of-the-road menu – comprising steaks, salads, pizza and pasta – account for Hatfield's established core of loyal regulars. You may well join their ranks. 129-131 Hatfield St, Gardens, 465 7387, open lunch Mon-Fri, dinner Mon-Sat.

### Kaapse Tafel ($$$)
Still going strong after 20 years the Kaapse Tafel delivers a fairly authentic taste of the Cape, with a menu of *bredies*, *bobotie*, Cape seafood dishes and mealie tart. The diner profile is dominated by tourists, peppered here and there by locals. 90 Queen Victoria St, Cape Town, tel 423 1651, open lunch Mon-Fri, dinner Mon-Sat.

### Kirstenbosch National Botanical Garden ($$)
Kirstenbosch's cavernous Silvertree Restaurant offers a fairly innovative menu – featuring the likes of ostrich and game – an impressive wine list, and good old fashioned service. The target market is clearly tourists but the tab is reasonable, given the gorgeous setting and attentive waiters. In winter make sure to hog a table near the roaring fire, in summer grab a seat outside under the watchful gaze of owls and other nocturnal creatures. Rhodes Avenue, Newlands, tel 762 9585, open daily lunch & dinner.

### Kotobuki ($$)
Some live on it, others detest it, but for many the taste of sushi is utterly addictive. Kotobuki resembles something along the lines of an airport departure lounge but the authentic Oriental and loyal local clientele speak of another experience: the sushi is a winner. 3 Avalon Centre, Mill St, Gardens, tel 462 3675.

### La Colombe ($$$)
Fine French dining on a beautiful wine estate a stone's throw from the city centre. On the same farm and also recommended is the Constantia Uitsig Restaurant (tel 794 4480), offering Italian-Mediterranean eating on both indoor and outdoor tables. Constantia Uitsig Farm, Spaanschemat River Rd, Constantia, tel 794 2390, open lunch & dinner Mon, Wed-Sat, dinner daily in season.

### Maestros ($)
Granted, with a menu dominated by red meat and gooey cheese sauce, this Cape Town institution will certainly not be everyone's first choice, but for a nostalgic trip back to the 80's and prices from a slightly later era, why the heck not? 60 Kloof St, Gardens, tel 423 0853, open daily for lunch & dinner.

### Mama Africa ($$)
Pitched mainly at tourists but also popular among locals, this vibey restaurant with a 12m bar in the shape of a green mamba lists an extensive range of dishes from across Africa. Marimba and Congolese groups are in the house every night except Sunday – the feet start tapping at about 8pm. 178 Long St, Cape Town, tel 426 1017, open for dinner Mon-Sat.

### Mr Pickwicks ($)
Mr Pickwicks has rescued many an urban nocturnal dweller from a debilitating attack of the munchies. More often than not it's buzzing and the food, piled high on tin plates, is guaranteed to plug any gap. Most popular are the footlong baguettes filled with interesting goodies. 158 Long St, Cape Town, tel 424 2696, open daily until the wee hours.

### Naked on Kloof ($)
On the Naked menu is a vast variety of innovative wraps – something along

the lines of a rolled pita bread stuffed with a delicious filling e.g. spicy Thai chicken. Naked's a good casual stop-off after a late-night movie at the Labia. 51 Kloof St, Gardens, tel 424 4748, open 9am-midnight.

### Nelson's Eye Restaurant & Grill ($$)
To many carnivores a plate without meat is but a plate of garnish, suitable for rabbits maybe but certainly not for real men. If you sympathise with this view, book a table at Nelson's Eye, a popular and cosy spot that has survived the ravages of Nouvelle Cuisine. 9 Hof St, Gardens, tel 423 2601, open lunch Mon-Fri, dinner daily.

### The News Café ($$)
Currently the place to be as far as the Atlantic flashset is concerned. An airy space spilling onto Green Point's main drag, the News Café is a popular venue for breakfast and lunch meetings, by night a loud throbbing hub to spot and be spotted. On weekends the 40 or so tables turn over fast and furious – for an intimate dinner go elsewhere. Breakfast, grills, sandwiches, smoothies and cocktails are on the menu lineup – all fairly priced and delivered with snappy service. Exhibition Building, 81 Main Rd, Green Point, tel 434 6196, open Mon-Fri from 7.30am, Sat & Sun from 9am.

### Ocean Basket ($)
Good seafood at good prices is the secret behind this local success story of several outlets and queues running halfway round the block. Inside, the service is zippy and the seafood tasty, with prices hovering between low and lowish. Outlets in Kloof St, Gardens (tel 422 0322), Tyger Valley Centre, Bellville (tel 914 5364), and cnr Main & Gabriel Rd, Plumstead (tel 761 0765). All are open daily, with Kloof Street definitely the best of the lot.

### On The Rocks ($$)
A spacious venue known for a grand postcard view of Table Mountain. The menu is standard and wide-ranging, covering everything from seafood to poultry and red meat. 45 Stadler Rd, Bloubergstrand, tel 56 1988, open Tue-Sat lunch & dinner, Sun lunch, closed Mon.

### Pizzeria Napoletana ($$)
Napoletana is as authentic as Italian comes: in the same family for some 40 years, grumpy proprietor, Italian TV channel blaring in the background, massive Sicilian murals and a weird mix of clientele. Veal parmigiano and tasty pizza and pasta are among the house specialities. An interesting glimpse into another world. 178 Main Rd, Sea Point, tel 434 5386, closed Mon.

### The Restaurant ($$$)
A relaxed, yet stylish modern brasserie on Green Point's Somerset Road, with a cutting edge menu described as "global fusion" – a creative hybrid of Eastern and Western influences. 51A Somerset Rd, Green Point, tel 419 2921, open dinner Mon-Sat.

### Vilamoura ($$$)
Overlooking the Camps Bay main drag, Vilamoura has acquired a reputation for dishing up the city's finest and freshest seafood – at the prices, one would expect nothing less! The service is a little stuffy but the decor is beautiful and the seafood superbly prepared and presented. The Promenade, Broadway Centre, Victoria Rd, Camps Bay, tel 438 1850, open daily for lunch & dinner.

### Wharfside Grill ($$)
Among the city's flagship seafood restaurants, the Wharfside Grill is a cavernous space filled with marine paraphernalia and wonderful views of the harbour and sea from most tables. Listed among other fishy items on the no-frills, just-good-food menu is a Fisherman's Basket loaded with mussels, linefish, prawns and calamari. Mariner's Wharf, Hout Bay, tel 790 2130, open daily for lunch & dinner.

### Wild Fig ($$)
On the same open grounds as Valkenberg Hospital in Observatory, the Wild Fig is a solid favourite among southern suburbanites seeking a satisfying meal out. The restaurant is cosy, the service is good and the menu is reliable and wholesome. Courtyard Hotel, off Liesbeeck Parkway, Observatory, tel 448 0507, open lunch Mon-Fri, dinner daily.

### Willoughby & Co ($$)
Restaurant in a mall but the seafood and sushi is professionally prepared and the service generally slick. The menu is chalked up on a board and the fish is served in the pan with potato wedges, rice or salad. A good quick-in quick-out option after a mad bout of Waterfront shopping. Victoria Wharf, V&A Waterfront, tel 418 6115, open lunch & dinner daily.

### Zero932
A pop-minimalist restaurant on Main Road, Green Point, that could well be mistaken for a sushi bar, but is in fact loosely modelled on a Belgian beer hall. Zero932 (essentially the dialling code to Belgium) features sharp design lines and an oddly traditional Belgian menu, with the emphasis on seafood in various guises, accompanied by no other than frites and mayo or stoemp (Belgian mash). Plus, there's a choice of 40 Belgian brews – seventh heaven for beer lovers or what? Exhibition Building, 79 Main Rd, Green Point, tel 439 6306, e-mail zero932@iafrica.com, open daily from 12 noon.

### Want to know more?
The above is a mere smattering of what exists on the Cape Town restaurant front. For further listings and reviews there are a number of useful publications, none particularly outspoken but otherwise comprehensive. Tony Jackman's *Cape on a Plate* (Guides for Africa) is the current favourite, with detailed reviews and restaurants arranged by theme and region. You'll find it at most bookshops. Published annually, Style Magazine's *Restaurant Guide* is fairly comprehensive and covers the Western Cape and the rest of the country. The V&A Waterfront publishes a free glossy guide to its 60 or so eateries – take the descriptions with a pinch of salt and you'll be okay. For a view from the horse's mouth get online and check out www.dine.co.za, a website loaded with uncensored (as far as we know) customer praise and gripes. Also check out the entertainment section of local newspapers – these frequently feature honest views on places good and bad.

## •rhodes memorial

Perched regally on the elegant slopes of Devil's Peak, Rhodes Memorial commands an amazing view of the Cape Flats, the Southern Suburbs and the distant rampart of the Hottentots Holland mountains. Built in honour of the arch-imperialist Cecil John Rhodes, the memorial itself is somewhat pompous, flanked by giant bronze lions and a triumphantly naked (bronze) horseman. Tasty, albeit pricey meals can be enjoyed at the adjacent tea garden (tel 689 9151, open 9am-5pm), and there are gentle strolls to be had above the Memorial. Head south towards Newlands Forest, or northward along the lower contour path to an inspiring vantage point over herds of wildebeest, zebra and the City Bowl. To get there, follow the signs from Rhodes Drive (M3) near UCT, Rondebosch.

# •robben island

Taking a trip to Robben Island is like poking your finger into a historical power-point. This desolate scrap of land was a crucial 'set' for one of the world's most inspiring political dramas, and the Island now carries huge resonance as a symbol of both injustice and democratic renewal. It's an absorbing place, which sheds a crystalline perspective on the country's progress, and pulsates with a meditative energy.

Ferries leave the Waterfront hourly (8am-3pm daily, R100 adults, R50 children, central booking tel 419 1300), and you can buy your tickets at the Clock Tower terminal, which also serves as the departure point. Tours take 3.5 or 4.5 hours, including sailing time: the best option is the longer, self-guided tour as there's plenty to see and you definitely don't want to rush. The trip out is about 30 minutes, on a hi-tech catamaran that might have been bought from a bankrupt Bond villain.

On arrival at Murray's Bay harbour, decide whether to start off with a bus tour around the island or a tour of the prison. The bus trip stops at several historical landmarks and gives a good sense of the island's lonely, windbitten geography. First up is the Muslim kramat, a beautiful shrine honouring a Malay holy man imprisoned here by the Dutch in the 17th century. You'll also pass a leper graveyard and a leper church designed by Sir Herbert Baker – the Island was a lepers' refuge in the early twentieth century. Further along the route is the notorious lime quarry, where Mandela and fellow inmates did hard labour in the sixties. Over the years the lime quarry became, with the help of sympathetic warders, a place for furtive study and debate.

The Prison visit begins with the Footsteps of Mandela tour through the famous B-Section. The guides are former inmates, and some are superb talkers. B-Section is a small compound of tiny cells and a building of huge historical significance: initially the scene of defeat for the liberation movement, it eventually became the transcendent and triumphant "struggle university." Mandela's cell is subtly signposted, but all the others are empty and anonymous; as sites of past incarceration they pose a quiet and affecting challenge to the visitor's imagination.

There's also an excellent exhibit called "Cell Stories" in the adjacent A-Section. Here the sparseness of prison life is deftly recreated; cramped isolation cells contain personal artefacts loaned by former prisoners, quotations, recordings and photographs. Take your time and let the recent past absorb you.

# •rock-climbing

When quizzed on his reasons for conquering Everest, Edmund Hillary tautly replied: "Because it's there." Table Mountain is undeniably "there", and local climbers have been answering its challenge for decades. From Lion's Head to Muizenberg and beyond, there are enough towering faces and cracks to make Spiderman dizzy. Certainly not a sport for gung-ho bravura in the bungy tradition, rock-climbing requires fitness, skill and care; in return you become part of a primal and poetic dialogue between nature and the human body. Beginners can polish their clambering skills with a guided climbing outing or joining up with an old hand.

**Blue Mountain Adventures**
Renowned climbing writer Tony Lourens offers guided rock-climbing outings tailored to your desires and level of experience. One-day climbs and scrambles on Table Mountain are the staple, but longer trips to the Cedarberg, Montagu and beyond can be arranged. All equipment is provided. Tel 439 8199, e-mail tonyblue@iafrica.com, website www.skyboom.com/bluemountainadventures.

**Venture Forth Rock Climbing**
If you've never climbed before or need to refresh your skills, Venture Forth conduct a fun one-day rock-climbing course. You're taught the basics of climbing equipment, knots, anchoring and belaying, with a bout of abseiling thrown in for good measure. Classes are taught on low-angle rock on Lion's Head, Table Mountain or Muizenberg. Tel 424 0116, cell 083-255 3466, e-mail dolby@iafrica.com, website www.venture-forth.com.

# •roller-blading

Roller-blading or inline skating as it is also known, is coolness on wheels. For those new to the sport it's also the potential embodiment of everything spectacularly uncool. The sport has come a long way since the squeaky supermarket skates of old and once you get the hang of things, the pavements and tarmac are a ticket to low friction freedom. Dress up in your best dayglo and join the trendy pundits of this growing fad along the smooth promenade running from Mouille Point to Sea Point. If you haven't got your own blades you can rent a pair from Rent 'n Ride, located in the same neighbourhood.

**Rent 'n Ride**
A friendly hire shop that, apart from rollerblades, stocks everything from bicycles to quad bikes to jet skis. For about R40 you can buy two hours of public admiration, impressive pirouettes and fast sprints down the Atlantic seaboard straight. 1 Park Rd, Mouille Point, tel 434 1122, e-mail bahamab@iafrica.com, open daily 10am to sunset.

**sandboarding**
**scenic drives**
**scratch patches**
**sex shops**
**shark diving**
**shopping malls**
**signal hill**
**skydiving**
**south african gallery**
**spectator sport**
**strip clubs**
**sundowners**
**surfing**
**survival games**
**swimming pools**

# •sandboarding

Have no snow, will sandboard! A shortage of powdery pistes in these parts has spawned a newfangled board sport on the towering sand dunes of the West Coast. For an aspirant snowboarder, a bout of sandboarding makes for an ideal (and cheap) crash course before hitting colder climes: the gear and the skills required are pretty similar. But sandboarding is attracting devotees as a thrillseeker's wet dream in its own right: the dune setting is dramatic, the sun is warm and the wipeouts are relatively painless.

**Downhill Adventures**
Downhill Adventures' sandboarding daytrips include transport to and from the dunes (an hour from Cape Town), use of equipment, expert instruction, and a full lunch. Overbeek Building, corner Orange, Kloof and Long St, tel 422 0388, e-mail downhill@mweb.co.za, website www.downhilladventures.com.

# •scenic drives

Not up to burning calories but need to get out and about? Then get behind the wheel, put foot to pedal and take a leisurely drive through a scenic segment Cape Town. A favourite CD, a sunroof, a full tank of gas and a pitstop for burgers and *slap* chips along the way will add further spice to this popular Sunday pastime.

### Cape Point

Taking the Main Road from Muizenberg, through Kalk Bay, Fish Hoek, Simon's Town and beyond, is a pleasurable coastal trip through a slice of Cape Town history. The drive is best scheduled first thing in the morning – any later tends to be a bumper to bumper experience in these suburbs. Constant ocean views, a road lined with historic buildings, coffee shops, junk-cum-antique shops and galleries, are the main attractions. The Natale Labia Museum in Muizenberg; Kalk Bay's Brass Bell, harbour and buzzing Olympia Café; Jubilee Square and the Marina in Simon's Town; and the penguins and restaurant at Boulders Beach, are but a handful of reasons to stretch your legs along the way. From Simon's Town the road enters open country, winding up to Cape Point and onward to Scarborough, the ethereal Misty Cliffs, Kommetjie and Noordhoek. At Noordhoek either head back to the city via Ou Kaapse Weg or, when re-opened, squeeze further pleasure along Chapman's Peak to Hout Bay.

### Chapman's Peak

An all-time family and tourist favourite Chapman's Peak sits high on the world's most scenic drive list. It is also among the most fragile settings, with rockfalls a fairly common event – as a result the pass has been closed until further notice. The drive is a thrilling 10km ribbon of tar cutting a tortuous path between vertical cliffs that drop into the angry ocean below. The views are unceasing and dramatic, taking in Hout Bay and the Sentinel at one end and Noordhoek's shimmering white beach at the other. A number of viewsites are provided along the way.

### Signal Hill

Always a pleasant early morning or sunset cruise, Signal Hill is a short drive filled with unfolding views of city, harbour and the Atlantic seaboard. Extend the experience with a leisurely picnic and a gentle stroll along the Lion's rump. Access to Signal Hill is from the top of Kloofnek Rd.

### Tafelberg Road

Best savoured at snail's pace, Tafelberg Road is a mirror image of the Signal Hill drive. Take a left at the top of Kloofnek Rd, snub the queues at the Cable Station and continue. Pull off at one of many viewpoints along the tranquil road and enjoy the vista of city and open ocean spreading out far below. Tafelberg Road ends about 5km later in a cul-de-sac and gives way to a fairly level jeep track that leads to the King's Blockhouse – a moderate walk worth leaving the car for.

## •scratch patches

Tiger's eye, malachite, blue-lace agate, jasper... and many more. Half of the planet's gemstone varieties can be found at Scratch Patch in Simon's Town and the V&A Waterfront, and for a very reasonable price you can fill bags with all the gleaming, mysterious pebbles you desire. At the Mineral World gemstone shops attached to both Scratch Patches a range of gemstone jewellery, gifts and artwork are on display. At the Simon's Town site you'll also find

Topstones, the world's biggest gemstone tumbling factory, where you can watch rough stone being polished. Simon's Town Scratch Patch, Dido Valley Rd, tel 786 2020, open Mon-Fri 8.30am-4.45pm, Sat-Sun & public holidays 9am-5.30pm; V&A Waterfront Scratch Patch, Dock Rd, tel 419 9429, open Mon-Fri 8.30am-4.45pm, Sat-Sun & public holidays 9am-5.30pm.

## •sex shops

Some people go to sex shops to expand their general knowledge in the fields of erotic technology and aesthetics, or to study the semiotics of arousal and postmodern gender fluidity, or simply to meditate on the intriguing architecture of physical love. Oh yeah?! Truth is, people go to sex shops to buy extremely rude objects for themselves and their friends. No arguing it, sex shops are fascinating places to spend a spare half-hour or two, places filled with a mind-boggling range of weird and bizarre paraphernalia, some of it best left to genital contortionists. And don't squirm if you bump into Auntie Iris or your new boss in the dildo department – chances are, they will be a lot more embarrassed than you.

### Adult World
Each of Adult World's four branches are smut superstores, stacked to the rafters with erotic magazines and videos, naughty lingerie and a truly eye-popping range of sex toys. There are luminous armies of vibrators in all shapes and sizes, gleaming parades of synthetic vaginas, and enough blow-up dolls to float the Titanic. Each branch stocks a sizeable collection of gay material. 51a Plein St, Cape Town, tel 461 3001; 36 Riebeeck St, Cape Town, tel 418 7455; 174 Main Rd, Claremont, tel 683 4414; 76 Voortrekker Rd, Bellville, tel 948 8125.

### The Hustler Shop
Same thing, different name, with an extensive range of equipment, visual manuals and latex simulations spread across five stores. 9a Marine Rd, Sea Point, tel 434 4697; 70b Voortrekker Rd, Bellville, tel 949 8188; 146 Voortrekker Rd, Parow, tel 930 7792; 31 Loop St, Cape Town, tel 419 8578; 235 Long St, Cape Town, tel 424 8267.

## •shark diving

Great White Sharks are the mobsters of the ocean, inspiring terror, revulsion and Hollywood blockbusters. They're also beautiful and extraordinary animals – and you can meet them in person (without risk to your person), by joining a shark diving expedition in Western Cape waters. The routine is simple: leap on a boat, head out to sea and watch carefully as the tour operators attract local Great Whites with the irresistible scent of mashed pilchards. Kitted out in scuba gear, you are lowered into the water inside a (strong) steel cage, where you can observe and take pictures as the toothy bruisers approach and sample the bait. Try resist commenting on their table manners.

### South Coast Seafaris
Cage diving, whale-watching, scuba diving and caving are all on the entertainment menu at Gansbaai. The shark-diving operation, off Dyer Island, supports the Stellenbosch University shark research programme. Daily transfers from Cape Town and backpacker accommodation are available. Gansbaai, tel 028-384 1380, e-mail seafaris@iafrica.com, website www.whitesharkdiving.com.

### White Shark Ecoventures
Operating from Gansbaai, White Shark Ecoventures offers a day tour to "Shark Alley", a protected channel between Dyer Island and Geyser Rock. Fine food, dive certificates, and transport to and from Cape Town are provided. An established, upmarket tour. Tel 689 5904, cell 083-412 3733.

### White Shark Projects
White Shark Projects runs a day tour from Kleinbaai, just east of Gansbaai. A substantial portion of the tour price is donated to the South African Great White Shark Research Institute. Tel 555 1060, cell 082-375 3472.

## •shopping malls

The Capetonian mall is a strange and wonderful animal. It's bigger than a blue whale and feeds on a nutritious plankton of credit cards and cheque-books. It has a skeleton of chrome, marble, escalators and towering plastic trees, and numerous vital organs that include multiplex cinemas, restaurants, ATMs and stores selling everything from fudge to designer luggage to solid gold kudus. No-one really knows why we spend so much time in shopping malls but the important thing to know is that malling is as much a spectator sport as it is about consumption, and you needn't actually buy stuff to enjoy yourself there. Amble past the gleaming displays and fantasise about future acquisitions. Watch the endless parade of humanity and the competing brands screaming out for your attention. Glide over the gleaming tiled floors and meditate to the gentle digital mantra of chirping tills and canned muzak…

### Canal Walk Shopping Centre

Shopping will never be the same! With a mind-boggling choice of 450 shops and 50 restaurants, a multimedia entertainment centre and the largest movie complex in South Africa, all housed in an awesome temple combining classic and post-modern architectural influences, the Canal Walk Shopping Centre in Century City is a tribute to the gods of mass commerce. While even the most zealous anti-capitalist will be left gobsmacked by the scale of things, not everyone will be up to sustaining the experience. So while mom wears the credit card thin dad and the kids can hijack a boat, head down the canals and climb the fence to Ratanga Junction. Century City (off N1), Milnerton, tel 555 4444, open daily.

### Cavendish Square

The original Cape Town mall, Cavendish is the natural habitat of well-heeled Southern Suburbs housewives, flexitimers and babbling clumps of off-duty teenagers. It's an opulent place, equipped with two cinema complexes, umpteen clothing stores and a domed glass ceiling that allows you to gaze at the heavens while standing on the escalator. Cavendish St, Claremont, tel 674 3050, open daily.

### Tyger Valley Centre

Tyger Valley's reputation as the retail mecca of the Northern Suburbs has been somewhat dented since the birth of Canal Walk, but it is nevertheless home to a huge range of shops and restaurants that serves an affluent, mainly white Afrikaans customer base. The architecture is pure mid-West Americana, with acres of timber and neon, and a truly gigantic movie screen in the food court. 1 Bezuidenhout Drive, Bellville, tel 914 1822, open from 9am.

### Victoria Wharf Shopping Centre

Cape Town's flagship waterfront shopping emporium, the Victoria Wharf throngs with foreign and upcountry tourists, not to mention half of the city's population over the holiday season. Restaurant and retail prices are heftier than elsewhere, but a steady flow of local consumers and mallrats courses through the Waterfront labyrinth. The adjacent dockside and gorgeous mountain views, make for first-class dawdling terrain. V&A Waterfront, tel 418 2369, open daily from 9am. (See also page 113)

# •signal hill

Signal Hill is the backside of the sphinx suggested by the silhouette of Lion's Head. It's an unglamorous hump of a hill, but it commands wonderful wide-angle views of the city, Sea Point and Table Bay: for a twinkly evening spot to make out in or quaff sundowners look no further than the parking lot at the end of the scenic road leading from Kloofnek. Nearby is the famous noon gun that has jolted Capetonians from their late-morning siestas for more than a century, and a sombrely atmospheric kramat (Muslim burial shrine) lies on the saddle between the Hill and Lion's Head.

# •skydiving

The earth is an intricate patchwork of green and brown fields, 11000 feet away. The plane's engine roars in your ears. You glance around at your fellow adventurers and in their strained expressions you recognise the question you've been asking yourself... "What the *&%#!! am I DOING?". Too late. Your time is up. You – and the experienced instructor you're strapped to – leap into the windy void. For several exquisitely insane seconds, you plummet at an ungodly speed towards the big round rock you know and love so well. Matters improve when your chute unfurls and you reach a happy compromise with gravity; for five minutes all is blissful peace and disbelief. Tandem skydiving is safe, easy, scary and utterly addictive. No training is required, and anyone in good health can do the drop thang.

**Skydive Citrusdal**

Best to book your tandem jump well in advance because believe it or not, jumping out of the sky is a popular pastime among Capetonians. Skydive Citrusdal charges by altitude: R650 for 9500 feet, R800 for 11000 feet; both options, like a certain beer, are best savoured slowly. Under-21's require parental consent. If you're keen on learning to jump alone, join Skydive Citrusdal's static-line courses conducted by expert jumpers every Saturday. Modderfontein Farm, Citrusdal (90 minutes drive from Cape Town), tel 462 5666, e-mail info@skydive.co.za, website www.skydive.co.za.

# •south african national gallery

For a bumper dose of visual, mental and emotional stimulation, use a few spare hours exploring the SA National Gallery (SANG), in the peaceful heart of Government Avenue. As the name implies, this is the country's premier art gallery, and the temporary and international shows mounted here are daring, varied and often inspiring. On a random visit to the SANG you might sample a cocktail of contemporary photojournalism, central African sculpture and Soviet poster art. Vibey and outrageous art events happen here on occasion: a recent bash called Soft Serve featured an authentic live boxing match in the courtyard, an impromptu hair salon, and a medley of certifiably loony performance artists. Not all of the gallery's permanent collection is on display but certain artworks are fixtures and should be sought out: Jane Alexander's profoundly unsettling plaster-and-bone sculpture of three fantastical figures, The Butcher Boys, and Willie Bester's Head North – a remarkable life-size ox created from machinery and miscellaneous found objects. Worth pausing at is a charmingly unprophetic 1897 painting titled Holiday Time in Cape Town in the Twentieth Century: this absurdly joyous Victorian fantasy resonates interestingly with the dynamic ferment of modern Cape Town. Works by Penny Siopis,

Cecil Skotnes and mysterious Namibian printmaker John Muafangejo are also on display, as well as an intriguing collection of European landscape and portrait painting, dating from the 1600's onwards. Complete your visit with a cuppa in the gallery's elegant coffee shop. Government Ave, Cape Town, tel 465 1628, e-mail sang@gem.co.za, website www.museum.org.za, open Tue-Sun 10am-5pm, entry R5.

## •spectator sport

The stadium is packed to the rafters, the sunshine kisses the green turf, the crowd groans with excitement as the first ball is kicked... For many Capetonians, watching live sport is a primal, exhilarating and addictive experience – a potent combination of theatre, warfare and religious observance. For others, it's a chance to be silly and shout a lot. While umpteen sports are played in Cape Town, only a handful are watched by more than one man and his dog. These are the options.

### Cricket
Ardently followed by a wide range of Capetonians, of all ages, races and genders. As any Pakistani bookmaker will tell you, Newlands Cricket Ground is where it all happens. Perhaps the most beautiful ground on Planet Cricket, Newlands lies nestled beneath ancient oaks and the imposing silhouette of Devil's Peak. Provincial, test and one-day international cricket matches take place here. One-day internationals are festive, good-humoured and often nailbiting. Five day test matches can be a little tedious, but if you're in the area during a match, drop in after lunch for a reduced price (normally R10). Find a grassy corner, have a beer and meditate to the sound of willow striking leather. 161 Campground Rd, Newlands, tel 674 4146.

### Rugby
To paraphrase Bill Shankly, rugby isn't a matter of life and death in the Western Cape – it's much more important than that. Provincial, international and Super 12 contests are fought at the impressive Fedsure Park (ex-Newlands Stadium). If Western Province or the Stormers (the Western Cape regional team) are on a winning run, get hold of a ticket. The stadium will be packed and the atmosphere will weigh heavy with testosterone. Go Breyton, go! Contact the Western Province Rugby Football Union, Boundary Rd, Newlands, tel 686 4955.

### Soccer
While it's not as well attended as cricket or rugby, Cape Town soccer is skilful and competitive. The most ambitious and professional club in the city is Ajax Cape Town, jointly owned by its Amsterdam namesake, which plays home games at Fedsure Park in Newlands. The best matches to watch are between a local team and either of the Soweto glamour boys, Orlando Pirates and Kaizer Chiefs, who draw a buzzing crowd wherever they go.

Matches are at Green Point Stadium, Athlone Stadium and Fedsure Park. Tickets for league matches are cheap at around R15 – book through Computicket outlets, tel 918 8910.

**Horse Racing**
The sport of kings takes place at Kenilworth, Milnerton and Durbanville racecourses. For specific info contact the Western Province Racing Club (tel 551-2110) or watch the press for details. If you can't tell one end of a horse from another, look no further than the annual J&B Met, the sexiest race in the country, which starts at 10am on the first Saturday of February at Kenilworth Racecourse. Dress to thrill.

# •strip clubs

Ever since the steamy day on which Salome performed the legendary dance of the seven veils, saucy and shapely women have been getting their kit off on stage. The act of stripping is a mysterious and powerful one, inspiring in the audience a fusion of lust, admiration and awe. You too can experience these confused emotions in a variety of Cape Town strip clubs. Unlike most big cities, Cape Town lacks a distinct erotica district – under the old sexually repressive regime, stripping was illegal. Nowadays, you'll spot beefy *platteland* boere lounging in city strip clubs, gleefully defying the Calvinist frowns of *dominees*, patriarchs and the *tannies* back home.

**Moulin Rouge Cabaret Bar**
One of Cape Town's largest and most respectable strip clubs, Moulin Rouge presents a titillating succession of nude cabaret strip shows from 1pm till past midnight. Table dancing, pole dancing and shower dancing (in which you watch girls showering!) are also on the bill of fare. You'll find a restaurant on the same premises. 40 Riebeeck St, tel 421 7147.

**Heaven**
A typical evening in Heaven is a gradual slide from tame to torrid. The stars work hard for their money and the evening is a fast succession of gyrating flesh. Like most strip clubs the decor is minimalist, little more than a bar counter and a small stage, and the menu features amateurs by day and pro dancers by night. An inevitable stop-off for hapless bachelors on a last night out with the mates. 164 Long St, tel 424 2140, R50 entry (R30 before 10pm).

# •surfing

From mellow beach breaks to cowabunga big wave fare, the Cape Peninsula has consistent varieties of most. It also offers the rare novelty of surfing two oceans in one day – if one set of rollers isn't up to scratch, chances are you will find satisfaction on the other side of the mountain. The beauty of surfing is that, apart from a wetsuit and a surf-board (or, boogie board), you don't need much fancy equipment – in fact, sticking with its purest form, body surfing, you can get away with nothing but a cozzie. A multitude of breaks can be experienced along the jagged Peninsula coastline, suited to pros and beginners alike, and working on just about any combination of wind, tide and swell. False Bay tends to be best for first-timers and ideal in north-westerly (NW) winds, while the Atlantic is more demanding – freezing water and bigger waves – and most effective in a south-easterly (SE) wind. The Cape Times carries a useful daily surf report, and local surf shops are happy to share their pearls. Bleach the hair, crank up the Beach Boys and prepare yourself for an ultimate union of body, board and foam.

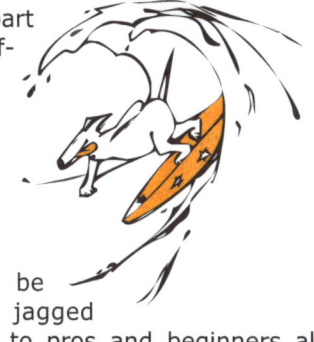

**Milnerton to Melkbosstrand**
For rolling beach breaks with postcard views of Table Mountain and Robben Island, the stretch from Milnerton to Melkbosstrand is a pleasure. The surf here works well on moderate swells and SE to NE winds the further north you go.

**Sea Point to Llandudno**
Below the Lion's rump Sea Point is Cape Town's answer to a more urban kind of wave action. Breaks like Thermopolye, Off-The-Wall and Queens Beach break on sedimentary reefs (booties advised), and work on modest to large swells and SE winds. Travelling south beyond the glitz of Clifton, Glen Beach, in the southern corner of Camps Bay, is a powerful little beach break that works in small to moderate swell with NE to SE winds. Even further south, in the shade of the 12 Apostles, Llandudno is a picturesque setting great for sundowners and potent beach break winders. On a larger swell, head towards the nudist beach of Sandy Bay and dare to surf buck naked.

**Noordhoek to Scarborough**
Moving down the Peninsula, Noordhoek is a long sandy beach offering plenty of hollow SE wind waves on a moderate swell – ideal for a contemplative walk-and-surf experience. Along to Kommetjie where the SW wind rules the waves, Long Beach is a consistent beach break and little brother to the formidable Sunset Reef that lies further out to sea – a big wave venue designed for the stout of heart. Closer to the village is Outer-Kom, a similarly challenging reef break, while opposite the crayfish factory at Soetwater is a wave which will happily oblige with a mouth of sea water and sand. Further south, Witsands and Misty Cliffs all work on N to NE winds, while at Scarborough you'll find quality waves on a SE offshore.

**False Bay**
Over to False Bay, Kalk Bay Reef is a sucking bowl of a wave that works best on a NW wind and on a moderate to large swell. It is also strategically placed in direct sight of the Brass Bell – a rare opportunity to impress

the beer-quaffing patrons with your skills. Close by is Fish Hoek, a great spot for beginners, though Muizenberg is where most neophytes can be found trying the surf thang. The rollers are long and mellow and as such, perfect for beginners and longboarders.

**Downhill Adventures**
If you haven't stood on a surfboard before, Downhill Adventures offer an opportunity to learn this finer art. Surfboards, wetsuits, hearty lunch and hands on theoretical and practical tuition by experienced instructors are provided. Just bring cozzie, towel and a determined streak. Tel 422 0388, e-mail downhill@mweb.co.za, website www.downhilladventures.com.

# •survival games

Survival games, apparently like war itself, are exhilarating. They're also an altogether more suitable and healthy alternative to the real thing. If you're a peace-loving citizen the idea of shooting your fellowman may not entirely gel. But feel rest assured, like chess or badminton survival games are acceptably PC – there is no real enemy and the bottom-line objective is simply to have loads of fun with a bunch of good friends or family. So if you've grown up on a steady diet of Nintendo or missed your SADF call-up, this is your chance for a glimpse into the heart of the hunter and the hunted.

**Action Paintball Games**
The world of *skop, skiet* and splat has never been this much fun. With Action Paintball Games you can spend half a day prowling around Tokai Forest – playing the lead in your own private Rambo movie. Bring a team, and splatter or be splattered. Paintball guns, face masks and bush jackets are supplied; all you need to bring is a cunning streak. 109 Albert Rd, Hout Bay, tel 790 7603.

**Laser Quest**
Playing Laser Quest lets you become a cunning trigger-happy space warrior for up to an hour – and few professions are as stimulating. You, your team-mates and opponents are armed with a chunky laser gun, dressed in a battle jacket studded with strategically placed targets, and set loose in a dim, labyrinthine battleground. Points are earned for shots on enemy targets, and deducted for shots conceded – at the end of the session, the players are ranked by the computer. This game is insanely addictive. Kenilworth Centre, Chichester Road, Kenilworth, tel 683 7296, open daily 10.30am-11pm (Sat 12pm), R20 per game; Shoprite Park, Voortrekker Rd, Parow, tel 930 2214, open daily (times vary).

# •swimming pools

Rumour has it that humans spent a couple of million years relaxing in the ocean between the evolutionary stages of monkey and *Homo sapiens*. This is presumably why we dig to swim, and why swimming is an optimal form of exercise – it doesn't cause injuries, and gets you fit all over. If you're in Cape Town and you feel like swimming lengths, a swimming pool is a wiser option than the Atlantic or Indian Oceans, which have no lane markings and are unreasonably long and cold.

### Long Street Baths
An oasis of habitable water in the middle of the city, this is one of few heated indoor pools in town. A cunning solution to the foul weather/exercise dilemma. On the same premises you will find a Turkish Bath with two steambaths, a plunge pool and a masseuse in attendance. Cnr Long & Buitensingel St, tel 400 3302, open daily.

### Muizenberg Pavilion
There are three pools – adult, slide and baby – to splash about in at this leisure complex appointed virtually on the beach in Muizenberg. A host of other facilities, including a supertube and putt-putt course, can be found close by. Avoid like the plague on Boxing Day and New Year's Day. Tel 788 7881, open daily, entry R7.50 adults, R4 children.

### Newlands Pool
An Olympic-sized unheated pool with a fine view of the mountain, a grandstand, and wide lawns for sunbathing and exercising children. If you feel like making a splash, make for the 5m diving board or the kiddies pool. Cnr Main & San Souci Rd, Newlands, tel 674 4197, open daily 7am-7pm (in season), entry R6 adults, R3 children.

### Sea Point Pavilion
Tucked right between the waves and the beachfront, and filled with bracing chlorinated seawater, Sea Point pool is ideal for a dramatic morning or sunset dip. Olympic-sized, with two paddling ponds and a dive pool nearby. Beach Rd, Sea Point, tel 434 3341, open daily 7am-7pm (7am-5pm in winter), entry R6 adults, R3 children.

**table mountain**
**ten-pin bowling**
**theatre**
**township tours**
**train trips**

# •table mountain

Vast, rectangular and ruggedly implacable, Table Mountain has a strong, silent personality which hovers somewhere between John Wayne, Frankenstein's monster and Buddha. It's perhaps the most distinctive hunk of rock on the planet, and over the centuries it has brought pleasure and succour to climbers, dogs, artists, escaped slaves, botanists, poets, bergies, abseilers, dassies and many others. The mountain's botanical wealth is incredible: this elevated patch of land is home to more endemic plant species than the entirety of the British Isles. Animals tend to keep a low profile, with the exception of various lizards and the dassie, or rock hyrax, a chunky rodent. A small population of nervous mountain goats roam the upper slopes.

The low-tech approach to climbing the mountain is still the best: its benefits include a mild to hefty cardiovascular workout, gradually unfolding panoramas, delicious mountain streams, and a truly spine-tingling moment when you step onto the summit. (See page 112 for route options.) Of the more than 300 routes, the most popular are Platteklip Gorge (from the city side), Skeleton Gorge (from Kirstenbosch) and Kasteelspoort (from the Camps Bay side). Bring sunblock, hats, waterbottles, a tasty lunch and some warm clothing. Avoid climbing alone, and don't climb if the weather is iffy: the mountain becomes dangerous when swamped by freezing grey cloud.

If you prefer climbing down or not climbing at all, the cableway offers a truly spectacular, sweat-free ascent. Because the cableway is the most famous tourist attraction in town many shun it as obvious and boring, but it's neither. The nightmare queues of old have been defeated by newfangled cable-cars, which carry more tourists more quickly. The cablecars rise from the Lower Station on Tafelberg Road and revolve as they glide upwards, affording 360-degree views for all. On arrival at the top, there are three easy walking routes, along which eleven viewpoints offer brain-fryingly dramatic vistas of Table Bay, the Atlantic coast, the Hottentots Holland mountains, and the Peninsula. The upper station boasts a smart restaurant, a bistro and a takeaway, and a shop with a fax and postal facility. Prices vary according to season and status: a student or pensioner taking the popular one-way option in winter pays only R20, while a return trip during high season (Dec-April) will cost an adult R75. During season, the first car up leaves at 8am, and the last car down leaves at 10pm. For more detail phone 424 8181.

## •ten-pin bowling

Ten-pin bowling is the archetypal middle-American leisure pursuit, bringing wholesome joy to rainy weekend afternoons for Archie and Jughead, Betty and Veronica and millions more. Bowling seems like a dull and artless pastime – until you first watch your own ball trundling down the aisle and casually obliterating the row of pins, in the manner of Obelix assaulting a phalanx of legionaries. From this instant the whole universe suddenly makes sense, and bowling becomes a complex, balletic, and breathtakingly athletic sport. Dig it.

### The Pines Entertainment Centre

At Pines you can bowl 365 days a year, from 9am to midnight. They've got 10 alleys, and plenty of bowling shoes for hire if you don't happen to own a pair – no bowling in conventional shoes allowed. There's also a full bar, a putt-putt course, big screen satellite TV, and pool tables. C5 Spilhaus Park, Jean Simonis Ave, Parow, tel 930 4795.

## •theatre

Just when Cape Town's theatre culture seemed to have kicked the bucket for good, up pops a couple of brilliant new plays and all the city's a stage. The runaway success of shows like Kramer and Petersen's Kat and the Kings (which had an award-winning run on London's West End) and the long-running bergie comedy Suip! has shown that originality can be lucrative. Directors such as Brett Bailey (Ipi Zombi), Fred Abrahamse and Marthinus Basson continue to push the creative envelope. And younger generations are switching on to the thrill of live dramatic entertainment. So get your backside into a theatre near you, and prepare to be stimulated... Excellent opera and ballet can be consumed throughout the year, while musicals and musical tribute shows are perennial favourites at the large theatres. Tickets range between R30 and R100 and bookings are through Computicket, tel 918 8950.

### The Baxter Theatre Centre

A huge face-brick theatre complex whose design, it has been said, was loosely based on Soviet Moscow's central railway station. A wide-ranging programme of shows are mounted here, including comedy festivals, jazz concerts and kiddie theatre. Rolling green lawns and water-features make for good impromptu picnics. Main Rd, Rondebosch, tel 685 7880.

### Evita se Perron

Evita Bezuidenhout, socialite, amateur politician and the most famous white lady in South Africa, has taken residence at her very own theatre-café at Darling railway station. Here you can sample traditional *platteland* food at Tannie's Station Cafe, drink at Bambi's Berlin Bar, and enjoy hilarious performances by Evita as well as Pieter-Dirk Uys' other alter-egos. Shows take place every evening during the festive season, and on weekend evenings through the year. An overnight stay at one of Darling's guesthouses is a fine option, particularly if you take up Evita's exclusive railway package trip. Contact the Perron for details and bookings. Darling Station, Darling (55 mins from Cape Town), tel 022-492 2851, e-mail evita@iafrica.com, website www.evita.co.za.

### Gauloises Warehouse

A new 280-seat venue with an impressive track record of promoting new plays. One of the few risk-taking, youth-oriented theatres in town, the Warehouse looks to ally theatre culture with club culture. More comfortable seats and insulation from the sounds of Green Point traffic will bring this aim a step closer. 6 Dixon Rd, Green Point, tel 421 0777.

## The Grange Theatre Café
An 80-seater restaurant and theatre space in the heart of Durbanville, catering to a predominantly Afrikaans audience with an irregular line-up of comedy bands, stand-up jokers, magicians and other off-beat artists. 1 Scher St, Durbanville, tel 976 7097, e-mail nfick@iafrica.com, open Wed, Fri, Sat (but phone ahead to make sure).

## High Street Theatre
Few forms of entertainment are neglected at the High Street Theatre, a new and dynamic 160-seat venue in the heart of the Northern Suburbs. The menu includes theatre, comedy, musicals, cabaret, and music ranging from blues and Kaapse hip-hop through to *platteland* crooners and chamber orchestras. Most performances are in Afrikaans. 19 Bella Rosa St, Rosenpark, Bellville, tel 914 7030, e-mail highstreet@mweb.co.za, website www.highstreet.co.za.

## The Little Theatre
A showcase for new work from the UCT Drama School. Some productions are superb, others self-indulgent. The drama school has a history of training fine actors such as Richard E Grant. University of Cape Town, 37 Orange St, Gardens, tel 480 7129.

## Maynardville Open-Air Theatre
January and February each year sees a Shakespeare comedy or tragedy staged under the summer sky in Wynberg's Maynardville Park. The leafy setting is genuinely romantic and the plays are mounted with great imagination by the best of Cape Town's designers and actors. Cnr Church & Wolfe St, Wynberg, booking through Computicket, tel 918 8950.

## The Nico Theatre Centre
In past decades the palace of state-funded white performing arts, the Nico has recently repositioned itself as a more popular, less elitist theatre. High-quality ballet and opera continues to be produced in the new era, while adventurous new dramas appear periodically. Don't be scared off by the sinister appearance of the building – nice things happen inside. DF Malan St, Foreshore, tel 421 5470.

## Oude Libertas Amphitheatre
A beautiful setting, good food and wine, and an annual schedule of music and drama make Oude Libertas a superb place to be on a summer's evening. The season begins in December and ends in March; book through Computicket, tel 918 8950. Ticket prices range between R30 and R60 – alternatively, for R8 you can picnic on the grass and hear the music but not see it. Opposite Stellenbosch Farmers Winery, Stellenbosch, tel 809 7000.

## Spier Wine Estate
Opera, theatre, jazz and comedy can be found at Spier's 1000-seater amphitheatre over the summer season (Nov-March). Most of the shows are locally produced, but international acts also feature. Spier boasts mountain views, manicured lawns, restaurants, cheetahs and a wine-tasting centre. Off Baden-Powell Drive, en route to Stellenbosch, tel 809 1100, e-mail info@spierarts.org.za, website www.spierfestival.co.za.

### The Theatre On The Bay

A swanky theatre patronised by a mature, well-heeled audience. Shows range from contemporary mainstream theatre and sex farces to musical tributes and revues. Try somewhere else if your tastes are experimental, but the productions here are polished and professional. 1 Link St, Camps Bay, tel 438 3300, e-mail toerine@netactive.co.za, website www.theatreonthebay.co.za.

## •township tours

Cape Town is a city steeped in a painful history, gradually emerging into a redemptive tomorrow – it vibrates with past and future simultaneously. This is most obvious in the townships of the Cape Flats, where entrenched poverty is juxtaposed with the new hope and energy of South African society. Visitors and curious locals can gain a glimpse of the past and experience the texture of Cape Flats life by joining an accredited township tour (or, cultural tour, as it is becoming known). Drop in at shebeens, spaza shops, nightclubs and street markets, and shoot the breeze with sangomas, musicians, activists and artists.

### Africultural Tours

Africultural Tours offer a jazz tour of the townships, visiting shebeens, taverns and jazz clubs. Also on the roster is a full-day tour of the astounding San rock art sites in the Cedarberg, and an overnight Slave Tour which traces the poignant history of slavery in the Cape. Tel 423 3321, e-mail actours@iafrica.com.

### Grassroute Tours

The "Beyond the Rainbow Curtain" tour offered by Grassroute Tours takes you through the Bo-Kaap and District Six, before heading out to Langa and Khayelitsha, and can be extended to include a trip to Robben Island. Also on the Grassroute roster is a novel "Culture of the Cape Fisherman" tour – which visitors spend a day with fishermen out at sea – and a half-day Bo-Kaap tour exploring Cape Muslim history and culture. Tel 706 1006, cell 082-951 1016, e-mail grasrout@iafrica.com, website www.grassroutetours.co.za.

### Legend Tours

Legend Tours run a half-day "Walk to Freedom" tour through the Bo-Kaap, District Six, Langa, Gugulethu, Nyanga, Mitchell's Plain, and the Samora Machel Housing Development Scheme. After lunch, an optional visit to Robben Island is offered. Tel 697 4056/7, cell 082-452 7879, e-mail info@legendtourism.co.za, website www.legendtourism.co.za.

### Tana-Baru Cultural Tours

For a guided journey through the Bo-Kaap (Malay Quarter) contact Tana-Baru. You can tour on foot or by car, and among the places visited are the country's oldest mosque, the Bo-Kaap Museum, various shrines, and the National Monument Strip. Also on offer is a half-day "Route of Many

Cultures" tour, which explores displaced communities in District Six and the Cape Flats. Tel 424 0719.

### Township Music Tours

Experience an evening of live township sounds, dancing, delicious home-cooked food and interactive music workshops in the company of Township Music Tours. Shebeens, jazz dens and private homes are on the route of this enchanting musical adventure. Book through Cape Tourism tel 426 4260, or phone your guide on cell 082-921 1126, e-mail muse-art@iafrica.com.

### Western Cape Action Tours

WECAT is a tour company run by former struggle activists, who take you into the heartland of Cape Town's township battlefields of yesteryear. The sites of the Trojan Horse and Gugulethu Seven shootings are visited, and the realities, hopes and legacies of contemporary township life are explored. Tel 461 1371, cell 082-721 9447, e-mail wecat@iafrica.com.

## •train trips

Cape Town's Metrorail train service may have its drawbacks, but it still offers a truly peaceful, low-stress way of getting from A to B. If A is Muizenberg and B is Simon's Town and it's a fine day, then you're in for one of the most gloriously scenic urban train rides on the planet. The False Bay railway hugs the shoreline so closely that at times the train feels like a long ocean-going yacht. Read, talk, daydream, feast your eyes on the glittering bay – and then repeat same on the return journey. A titbit of advice though: hide the Rolex and any other valuables and avoid travelling after dark. Alternatively, rustle up a group of 20 friends and book Metrorail's all-new chaperoned Tourist Coach, complete with guide and beefed up security, and follow the line to False Bay, the Winelands and other country destinations. Timetables and prices are available from Metrorail, tel 449 4045.

### Spier Vintage Train

The Spier Vintage Train is an elegantly fitted steam train which makes regular day trips to Darling, the Spier Wine Estate and Simon's Town – a refined and refreshing dose of old-school locomotion and magnificent scenery. The train is equipped with two fully-stocked bars, but does not serve food. All three outings begin and end at the lovingly restored Monument Station in Cape Town. The 2.5hr trip to Darling includes a ticket to a matinee performance at Evita se Perron on Darling Station, as well as a delicious picnic basket from Spier Wine Estate to munch en route. The scenic Spier and Simon's Town legs both take about an hour each way. Contact Monument Station for details and bookings, tel 419 5222 or 809 1100, e-mail spier7@iafrica.com, website www.spier.co.za.

walks
waterfront
whale-watching
windsurfing
wine routes
world of birds

## •walks

The scope to go up, down, sideways and around the Peninsula mountain chain is huge. Table Mountain alone has a rumoured 300 possible routes to the summit, while Tokai Forest, Silvermine Nature Reserve, Cape Point and all the rolling hills in between are loaded with blister potential. The following routes serve as a mere introduction, a fruit salad of Cape classics, popular urban sidewalks, forest and beach walks. The walks are tailored to a morning or afternoon and each can be completed within three hours or less. Hikes we shall leave to the masochists. Although the walks are mostly easy going, deviating from the marked path can have unpleasant side-effects, including the embarrassing attention of rescue teams. In other words, try stick to the beaten track.

### Bo-Kaap (urban)
A last chance to catch the real thing before the yuppies take over. Bo-Kaap should be explored on foot, but until you get to know it better, you will feel more comfortable joining an organised tour to the museum, a mosque, local homes and the ancient burial ground. Bo-Kaap Guided Tours (tel 422 1554) or one of several other operators can tell you more. Spread across the slopes of Signal Hill and pervaded by a strong history and community spirit, the Bo-Kaap neighbourhood is one of Cape Town's quaintest, featuring brightly painted terraced houses, narrow cobbled alleyways and views over the city.

### Cape of Good Hope Nature Reserve (mountain/coastline)
The Cape of Good Hope Nature Reserve has several easy to moderate walks peppered with a bit of everything: fynbos, coastal cliffs, baboons, shipwrecks, old cannons and blockhouses, rare African black oystercatchers and bontebok. And of course, damn fine views from beginning to end. The Olifantsbos (Shipwreck) walk, about 6km long, includes a rocky shoreline strewn with the shattered remains of the Liberty ship Thomas T Tucker – the skipper thought he was off Robben Island! Another easy walk is the Hoek van Bobbejaan, a 5km circular stroll that leads to another shipwreck and sightings of tortoises and rock lizards, while the 6.5km Kanonkop is a leisurely climb through fynbos to a cannon and wide-lens vistas. Entry by R20 permit (children R5), tel 780 9100, open daily 7am-5pm, 7am-6pm in summer.

### City Walk (urban)
Cape Town's city centre still sports a surprising number of old buildings in the local style loosely characterised as Cape Dutch, and the only way to get a close-up view of them is by plodding the pavements. A good place to start

is at the south end of Government Avenue (the end nearer the mountain) and amble down the altogether pleasant Company Gardens towards Adderley Street. The Gardens are flanked by an impressive concentration of buildings of historical, contemporary and architectural interest – among the more notables are the Houses of Parliament, St George's Cathedral, Tuynhuys, South African library, South African National Gallery, South African Museum and the Planetarium. Most of these are open to the public. The rest of the city centre is architecturally more disparate. Down Adderley Street and left into Strand, you will pass Koopman's De Wet House, a typical 18th century house, as well as the Lutheran Church and Martin Melck House. Up into Long Street, the area around Greenmarket Square is interesting and vibey – apart from the cobbled Square itself, the surrounding buildings, among them The Old Town House and Metropolitan Methodist Church are fine specimens from days gone by. (See also page 7 for an architectural overview.)

### Constantia Nek (forest/mountain)

Leave your car at Constantia Nek (opposite the restaurant), and join the Sunday regulars and their hounds on this pleasant amble through cool pine forest. Several forestry tracks intersect the plantation and the choice is yours to stay on the relative level towards Kirstenbosch or follow the road upwards. Taking the up route rewards with an altogether more independent experience, wonderful views, and the satisfaction of "I did it!" After inspecting the dams at the top for leaks, find a shady spot to enjoy your peanut butter sarmies, before dropping down the same way. No permit is required.

### Green Point (urban/coastline)

Green Point offers interest on both sides of Beach Road, starting from the Portswood Road end, just outside the Waterfront. It includes the 'Elizabethan' New Somerset Hospital (1860's), Fort Wynyard (spot the gun muzzles), Granger Bay marina, the wreck of the mailship Athens that sank in 1865 (only the engine remains), and the Green Point lighthouse, built in 1824 and which Capetonians insist on calling 'Mouille Point lighthouse'. Parts of the scene are a trifle bleak, but it's all level and fairly bracing, with a number of caffeine spots along the way.

### Kirstenbosch Botanical Garden (forest/mountain)

Kirstenbosch offers everything from a Braille trail to several serious slogs to the summit of Table Mountain. If your physical state falls somewhere between these extremes stick to the Silvertree Trail (forested ravines), the Yellowwood Trail (leading to a pretty waterfall in Skeleton Gorge) and the Stinkwood Trail, all three little more than invigorating strolls. These walks in the bag, you might like to plan an expedition up the steep slopes of Skeleton Gorge, popping out an hour or two later on the saddle between Devil's Peak and Table Mountain. The quickest return is either the same way (not particularly pleasant), or down Nursery Ravine, about 30 minutes walk from Skeleton Gorge. 70 Rhodes Drive, Newlands, tel 799 8899, open throughout the year, 8am-6pm winter, 8am-7pm summer, entrance fee R15 adults, R5 children.

### Jagers Walk, Fish Hoek (urban/coastline)

Fish Hoek may be known as the dullest retirement village in the Cape, but the good beach and pleasant Jagers Walk are adequate compensation. Jager's Walk starts at the beach (near the Fish Hoek Galley restaurant) and tracks the rocky coastline as far as Sunny Cove. From here the walkway continues unpaved for about 5km to Simon's Town. Time it right (Sept-Oct) and you'll more likely than not see whales frolicking in the bay.

### Lion's Head (mountain)

An obligatory climb for anyone remotely interested in the great outdoors. Lion's Head summit is only about an hour from the carpark off the Signal Hill road, along a well-built path and an optional clamber up a chain ladder. From the top, sea and city fill an unforgettable 360-degree panorama, at its best as the sun sets. For a novel variation time your walk for full-moon and join the queues up the hill, settling down to an early picnic supper at the top and descending by ethereal lunar light. No permit required.

### Newlands Forest (forest)

A favourite venue among late afternoon joggers, walkers and their hounds, Newlands Forest extends up the mountain above Rhodes Drive (M3) in Newlands. There's an extensive network of paths and a choice of easy and mostly shady circular walks passing through alien blue gum, pine, oak and patches of indigenous vegetation. Given the maze of crisscrossing paths it is difficult to describe, never mind follow, a specific route. But remember: home is down and most paths lead there. One option passes the excavated site of Paradijs and the remains of the Master Woodcutter's house, built in the early 18th century, others cross small streams that transform into raging torrents during the winter rains. All options start from the carpark at Newlands Forestry Station along Rhodes Drive. No entry permit required.

### Noordhoek Beach Walk (beach)

Sunday morning, head groggy, another week looming large... Noordhoek is an instant pick-me-up. Striding the length of this desolate beach on a perfect morning borders close to an esoteric experience and is also an opportunity to experience the very thing lacking in the average new millenium diet: wide open space. Interest is added to the walk by a visit to the jutting ribs and boiler of the Kakapo – a steamer that met its fate exactly a century ago during a maiden voyage to New Zealand – a dive into the Atlantic's icy waters, and leisurely breakfast at the nearby Red Herring, Café Adagio, or Noordhoek Farm Village.

### Pipe Track (mountain)

An easy and popular walk among local walkers (and the occasional mugger!), the Pipe Track runs more or less level for about 7km from Kloof Nek along the slopes of the Twelve Apostles above Camps Bay. The rewards include enormous views over the Atlantic coast, achieved at minimum physical effort. Several side tracks convert into serious climbs, so best ignore them. To start the walk, park at the designated area at the top of Kloof Nek Road (M62) and cross over towards the Camps Bay side of the mountain where you will find a sign and the path. No permit required.

### Sea Point Promenade (urban/coastline)

Sea Point beachfront or 'the Promenade' as it's locally known, leads one on the level from Three Anchor Bay to Bantry Bay. Moving back and forth between each end is an interesting mix of young, old, rich, poor, gloss and sleaze. Less a place to be seen than a place to see, Sunday afternoon on the promenade is a rich slice of Cape Town humanity. Other than the fascinating stew of fellow strollers, the more obvious family attractions include a playpark, a miniature train, putt-putt, the Sea Point swimming pool and postcard sunsets. End your outing either with an ice-cream on the pavement, or in style with an all-you-can-eat buffet tea at the Radisson Hotel (ex-Villa Via), or espresso and brownie at the sociable Newport Café and Market, both along Beach Road in Three Anchor Bay.

### Simon's Town (urban/coastline)
St George's Street in Simon's Town traces the seafront from the railway station and offers access to the Residency Museum, St Francis' Church, the SA Navy Museum, a Toy Museum and Jubilee Square. Old facades invite inspection and its fun to speculate on whether the old cableway really will be restored. An easy stride interrupted by several pleasant coffee stops.

### Silvermine Nature Reserve (mountain)
For maximum return with minimum investment, Silvermine is the way to go. Most of the walks in this popular and picturesque reserve perched high above Ou Kaapse Weg are easy-going, and even the most sedentary couch potato should be up to a stroll. Even if it's only a quick lap around the reservoir, with a braai to celebrate. For something a little more ambitious, Noordhoek Peak is an easy three-hour circuit almost entirely along gravel roads and rewarded with a stunning view of Hout Bay from the summit. Enter the reserve at the top of Ou Kaapse Weg. Tel 789 2455, open 8am-6pm summer, 8am-5pm winter, R5 entrance fee (& R10 per vehicle).

### Table Mountain (mountain)
Of the 300 or so possible low-tech routes to the top of Table Mountain, Platteklip Gorge, accessed left of the lower Cable station is the most popular – followed closely by Skeleton Gorge (above Kirstenbosch) and Kasteelspoort (from the Camps Bay side). The associated benefits of a trek up the Big Mother include a mild to hefty cardiovascular workout (depending on your fitness level), gradually unfolding vistas of the city and a spine-tingling moment when you step onto the summit. Although Platteklip Gorge is a straightforward upward slog be prepared – sunblock, a hat, adequate water, warm clothing and a packed lunch should be standard items in your backpack. Also, avoid climbing alone, and don't climb if the weather is iffy: the mountain is a temperamental old lady who doesn't take kindly to fools. At the top reward yourself with a snack at the Upper Cable Station restaurant and a one-way ticket home. No permit required.

### Tafelberg Road (mountain)
Why drive Tafelberg Road when you can walk it and simultaneously enjoy at your leisure an incredible vista of city and open ocean? Past the queues of the lower Cable station, the road is quiet, the gradient gentle and the view constant. The tarred section of Tafelberg Road ends about 5km later in a cul-de-sac, but from here you can continue on foot along a contoured jeep track that leads to the King's Blockhouse above Rhodes Memorial and the southern suburbs. No permit required.

### Tokai Forest (forest/mountain)
Elephant's Eye cave on Constantiaberg is at the end of a zigzag path – most of it fairly steep and without shade – leading up from the arboretum in Tokai Forest. The view at the top is well worth the sweat. Take drinking water with you and stop to admire the Tokai homestead (1796) where a ghostly horse and rider are reputed to appear every New Year's Eve. To access the start of this popular walk, take the M3 highway southwards towards Muizenberg, exit at the Retreat/Tokai offramp, double back under the highway and follow Tokai Road to its end. Tel 712 7471, entry free to walkers.

**Want to know more?**
If you're fat, unfit or long in the tooth, Mike Lundy's *Easy Walks in the Cape Peninsula* (Human & Rousseau) is for you. Packed between the covers are detailed instructions to 52 walks (one for every weekend of the year), most of them on the level and none longer than three hours duration, precise route maps and interesting bits and pieces of local lore. For foot-slogging of a more strenuous nature, refer to Lundy's *Twenty Walks around Hout Bay, Best Walks in the Cape Peninsula* and, *Weekend Trails in the Western Cape*.

## •waterfront

A winning union of water, air, earth and retail, the V&A Waterfront is Cape Town's leisure capital. It's more spacious and urbane than a suburban mall, with great views and bracing air. At the Waterfront you have options. See a movie at one of two cinema complexes, enjoy live jazz, buskers and clowns, or gawk at ragged-toothed sharks in the Two Oceans Aquarium. Crash on a quayside bench and commune with the Cape fur seals and gulls. Buy a kite, a bottle of champagne or a wedding ring. Choose from a lifetime's worth of music, clothing, books or crafts. Take a sunset cruise or a helicopter flip, or hunt for gems at the Scratch Patch. Food is in abundant supply, with takeaway joints and restaurants serving everything from fish 'n chips and hamburgers to haute cuisine. Food and drink can be a little strenuous, particularly in the smarter restaurants, but the convenience and breezy ambience of the Waterfront compensates. Tourists dig it, and locals dig it too. Waterfront Visitor Centre, tel 418 2369, website www.waterfront.co.za, open daily from 9am.

## •whale-watching

Few are unmoved by the sight of whales. They are creatures of mythic significance, surfacing repeatedly in our dreams, art and literature. In one sense they are closely related to us as intelligent mammals, but they're also utterly mysterious – vast yet exquisitely formed, singing eerily to each other on their deep-sea travels, whales make humans seem frantic, puny and banal by comparison. To admire these beasts, grab a pair of binoculars and head to the False Bay coast, Hermanus and West Coast between early August and late October, when Southern Right whales leave the open ocean for maternity leave in sheltered bays. Males make cameo appearances in the earlier weeks of the season, but the rest of the show belongs to females and calves. The rare and definitive highlight of any whale-watching experience comes when a particularly gleeful whale, by some miraculous culmination of forces, propels its body clean out of the water and returns with a giant blossom of spray. This antic is called "breaching" and it will make you yell inarticulately and hop about.

### False Bay
Not as many whales hang out in False Bay as in Hermanus, but you're still likely to see gratifying performances in September from Boyes Drive, a beautiful road which skirts the mountainside between Lakeside and Kalk Bay. Boulders Beach near Simon's Town is sometimes blessed with close-up appearances, while the high road between Simon's Town and Smitswinkel Bay offers fine vantage points.

### Hermanus
Touting as the Cape's Riviera, Hermanus offers some of the world's best land-based whale-watching. In season the stretch of clifftop walkways between New Harbour and Grotto Beach is a sure bet. Daily sightings are practically guaranteed in September and October. You'll find whale information signboards at the best lookout points and keep an ear out for the official Hermanus Whale Crier, who announces recent sightings by blowing a kelp horn. If you'd prefer a quieter whale-watching experience, any bit of steep coastline in the Walker Bay area will do. An especially fruitful lookout is at the little hamlet of De Kelders, 30 minutes drive further up the coast from Hermanus. For an up to the minute account phone the whale hotline (083-910 1028), or the Hermanus Info office on 028-312 2629.

### West Coast
Yzerfontein, a small and somewhat boring holiday village off the R27, is your best and closest bet for spotting whales along the West Coast. The bay provides a sheltered sanctuary that whales use for mating and calving. The best viewing months are from the end of June to September and for the purpose you'll find a MTN-sponsored station on the cliffs overlooking the bay. Apart from whales, Yzerfontein has an endless open beach tailored for walking, swimming and surfing. The island in the bay, known as Meeurots (Gull Rock) is home to a large seagull colony, while 10km further out to sea is Dassen Island. Yzerfontein's info office is waiting to tell you more, tel 022-451 2366.

### Want to know more?
*MTN Whale-Watch: A Guide to Whales and Other Marine Mammals of Southern Africa* (Struik New Holland Publishing), contains just about everything you need to know about whale-watching in the region, from a history of the whale industry to a detailed profile of some 44 different marine mammal species, an overview of the best viewing sites, the best times to catch different species in action, and a host of other attractions in each region.

## •windsurfing

Cape Town has reared several world-class windsurfing pros, and the city is spoken of in reverent tones by enthusiasts worldwide. The Cape Doctor must take much of the credit here: when the rest of us are cussing and clutching our hats in the summer south-easter, windsurfers are rushing to beaches and vleis around the peninsula, sporting mile-wide grins. This ain't an easy sport to master – but once you've got the hang of it, you slot into a moving high-energy sandwich of sea and wind. The experience is exhilarating, whether you're leaping off waves or blasting across flat water.

### Cape Sport Centre
At Cape Sport Centre in Langebaan you can get expert windsurfing tuition or do your own thing with a range of boards, rigs and wetsuits available for hire. The lagoon is truly beautiful, and when the wind is mild in the morning, conditions are ideal for beginners. Langebaan Lagoon, tel 022-772 1114, cell 082-658 1114, e-mail cwsa@iafrica.com, website www.capesport.co.za.

### SA Windsurfaris & Rentals
Join Grant Ross of Windsurfaris in a quest for the ultimate wave. In summer you'll find him on Blouberg beach, hiring everything you need to windsurf at sea, including boards, rigs, sails and wetsuits. And for both the neophyte and wave supremo, Windsurfaris offers practical courses in the art of staying upright in adverse conditions. Tel 082-449 9819, e-mail windsurf@iafrica.com.

## •wine routes

Visiting the Winelands of the Cape is like entering a sensory utopia – a magical zone where everything looks good, smells good and tastes good. The Stellenbosch, Paarl and Franschhoek valleys are dramatic arenas of mountain and farmland, in which the hard, wild geology of the surrounding peaks strikes a contrast with the soft, multihued patchwork of the vineyards and pastures below. Scattered throughout the green valleys are elegant whitewashed farmhouses in which some of the best wines on earth can be sniffed, sipped and savoured. Other crucial elements in the Winelands experience are sweet clean air, delicious food, and an atmosphere of contented sun-drenched peace. There's real pleasure to be had here. Each of the Constantia, Stellenbosch, Paarl and Franschhoek wine routes merit a full day's exploring. Listed below are estates that boast fine architecture, views, or food – in addition to good wine. Most estates charge between R5 and R10 for a wine-tasting session. In some cases this is refunded against the purchase of wine, which is sold by the case at tempting prices.

## •CONSTANTIA ROUTE

The Constantia estates are the cradle of the Cape wine industry, and were first cultivated by the wealthy burgher Simon van der Stel in 1685. On his death in 1712, his land was divided into three estates, Groot and Klein Constantia and Buitenverwachting. All three are beautifully appointed farms with exhilarating views, and all three continue to produce superb wine.

### Buitenverwachting

At the environmentally-aware Buitenverwachting, a committed team of ducks patrols the vineyards for snails. The estate's labour policy is similarly progressive: workers are well housed and contribute to management. But Buitenverwachting is most famous for its pleasant grounds, excellent wine and one of the country's best restaurants. Order a luxury picnic lunch from the restaurant (tel 794 1012) and enjoy an exceptional *dejeuner sur l'herbe* on the lawn. The best wines to taste are the flagship whites, Buiten Blanc and Rhine Riesling. Klein Constantia Road, tel 794 5190/1, tasting 9am-5pm weekdays, Sat 9am-1pm, cellar tours by appointment.

### Groot Constantia

The biggest and grandest of the Cape Town estates, Groot Constantia boasts graceful buildings, beautiful gardens and traditional Cape food at the Jonkershuis Restaurant. In the Manor House, built in 1692, you'll find a fine collection of antique furniture, ceramics and art. You can take a tour of the estate's production cellars (booking advisable) or just savour the results in the Bertrams Cellar tasting room. All of Groot Constantia's wines are of top quality, but the Gouverneurs Reserve and Weisser Riesling are recommended. Tel 794 5128, open 10am-5pm daily (later in summer), closed Christmas Day, New Year's Day & Good Friday, cellar tours and wine tastings daily.

### Klein Constantia

Regally overlooking the Constantia valley and the gleaming expanse of False Bay, Klein Constantia is one of the Cape's more beautiful wine farms. Excellent white wines are made here, but the estate's signature drink is the celebrated Vin de Constance, a delicious dessert wine that repeatedly caressed the palates of Napoleon, Bismarck, and Frederick the Great, and featured in the novels of Austen and Dickens. Give it a try. Tel 794 5188, open 9am-5pm Mon-Fri, 9am-1pm Sat.

### Steenberg Vineyards

The oldest wine estate in the country, Steenberg is set on a fine stretch of mountainside that was granted to a young widow, Catherina Ras, in 1682. The original buildings have now been restored, and the estate tastefully developed with an 18-hole golf course, an exclusive housing development and a handsome country hotel. Wines to sample include the merlot, the semillon and the chardonnay. Tel 713 2211, open Mon-Fri 8am-4.30pm (year round) & Saturdays 9am-1pm (Sept-April).

## •FRANSCHHOEK ROUTE

Three things make Franschhoek tick: food, scenery and wine. The last has been the district's lifeblood for centuries, but recently this dozy town has become home to many of the Cape's best restaurants. Lying at the head of a deep and well-watered valley, Franschhoek is blessed with outrageous mountain views on three sides. The town is saturated with tourists on weekends, so it's best to visit on an off-season weekday for a sumptuous meal, a rustic stroll and a bout of premium wine-tasting. Franschhoek's 17th-century Gallic heritage is documented in the Huguenot Museum in Lamprecht Street, near the baffling triple-arched Huguenot Monument. Several of the 20 wine estates are virtually in town or easily accessible by foot or bicycle. For more detail phone the Info office on 876 3603, or the Vignerons de Franschhoek hotline, tel 876 3062. (See also page 34 for Day Trip info.)

## Boschendal

Boschendal is the best-known wine farm in Franschhoek, and one of the oldest in the country – it was granted to the Huguenot settler Jean le Long in 1682. Today it belongs to the Anglo-American Corporation, and its oak-lined avenues, comely Cape Dutch buildings, stylish restaurant (tel 870 4274) and famous Pique Nique under fragrant pine trees, draw busloads of visitors. Most importantly, Boschendal produces an impressive range of red and white wines, which can be sampled at the Taphuis (tel 870 4211). Vineyard and cellar tours are available. Open daily, tastings Mon-Sat 8.30am-4.30pm (Sun in high season).

## Cabriere Estate

The Haute Cabriere Cellar Restaurant commands a fine view of the Franschhoek valley and its happy customers can order choice wine by the glass, and order half portions of excellent meals – thus allowing them the sensual pleasure of various combinations of food and wine. On Saturdays the estate's owner Achim von Arnim guides visitors through his cellars and may even demonstrate the gallant art of slicing the neck from a bottle of bubbly using a sabre. Tel 876 2630, open weekdays 8.30am-5pm, Sat 10.30am-1.30pm, tastings twice daily, closed Sun.

## Chamonix

The Chamonix estate has several strings to its bow: an award-winning gourmet restaurant, a fruit schnapps distillery, superb bottled water drawn from the farm's spring (Eau de Chamonix), and of course, a smallish but satisfying selection of wines. Tasting is in the Blacksmith's Cottage and cellar tours are by arrangement. Tel 876 2494/8, La Maison de Chamonix Restaurant, tel 876 2393, wine tastings Mon-Sun 9.30am-4pm, restaurant closed Mondays, Sunday evenings.

## Dieu Donné

Dieu Donné's position on the high western slopes above Franschhoek affords it panoramic views. Moreover, it slows the ripening of the grapes, thus ensuring subtle, balanced wines. More than 90% of Dieu Donné's output is exported. This estate is worth visiting for the sake of both eye and palate. Tel 876 2493, open Mon-Fri 9.30am-4.30pm, Sat 9.30am-12.30pm.

## Haute Provence

About 1km out of town, Haute Provence is renowned for producing Angel's Tears – a superb sweet-dry white blend – and several other products that have won international plaudits in recent years. It's a relaxed, hospitable place, shaded by towering oaks, and the comfy tasting room is decorated with quality South African oil paintings. Tel 876 3195, open daily 10am-5pm.

## La Motte

Credited as the estate that demonstrated the Franschhoek valley's potential to produce exceptional red wines, La Motte is well equipped for visitors with an immensely stylish tasting room. La Motte's wines have won a hatful of international medals and should be sought out, particularly the very popular Millennium red, a Bordeaux blend. Tel 876 3119, open Mon-Fri 9am 4.30pm, Sat 9am-12pm, closed Sundays, religious holidays.

### L'Ormarins
Probably best known for its Optima Reserve, this aesthetically pleasing high-tech estate has a wide range of other full bodied reds and well-balanced whites. A plush marble-lined tasting room, classic Cape Dutch architecture and a backdrop of golden vines creates a pleasant stop-off. Tel 874 1026, open Mon-Fri 9am-4.30pm, Sat 9am-12.30pm.

### Mont Rochelle
Established in 1688, Mont Rochelle is one of the best appointed estates in Franschhoek, known for 'cheap and cheerful' plonk. In the smart and elegantly decorated cellar – a converted Victorian fruit-packing shed – you can taste from the respectable Rochelle and Petite Rochelle ranges of whites and reds. Light lunches and picnic hampers are available as are horseback tours with Mont Rochelle's Equestrian Centre (tel 083-300 4368). Tel 876 3000, open Mon-Sat 11am-5pm.

## •PAARL ROUTE
Named after the great big lumps of granite that protrude from the nearby mountain, Paarl (the Pearl ) is an old, prosperous, somewhat boring place. The town's main claim to fame is being the official birthplace of Afrikaans, which is celebrated by an Afrikaans Language Museum and the self-important Taal Monument. Nelson Mandela stayed close by during his last years of imprisonment, in a cosy warder's house in Victor Verster prison; between wine farms you can stand outside the gates and reflect on the morning of February 11, 1990, when Madiba strolled hesitantly to an unknown future. Other than this, Paarl's main drawcards are its beautiful wine route and rich architectural heritage of many fine Cape Dutch, Victorian and Georgian buildings. For general info contact the Paarl Tourism Bureau (tel 872 3829), or, for specific wine route queries, phone 872 3605. (See also page 34 for Day Trip info.)

### Fairview
A lively and tourist-oriented estate, Fairview is famous for its goat-manned tower, which serves as the emblem on Fairview wine labels. An intriguing range of cheeses are made here – using cow's milk, goat's milk and even sheep's milk – and these can be bought at the estate's deli. Fairview has also been producing superb wine for centuries and according to legend, doctors of old prescribed teaspoons of Fairview poison to sick children. What with tour buses and families, Fairview can get a little hectic in summer, so it's not a bad idea to phone ahead for a crowd update. Tel 863 2450, open Mon-Fri 8.30am-5pm, Sat 8.30am-1pm.

### KWV
The cellar complex of the KWV (Kooperatiewe Wijnbouwers Vereeniging) covers 22 hectares – it's an immense cathedral to the gods of the grape, and the largest co-operative cellar known to man. As you are guided along aisles of giant vats, the atmosphere of fermentation and maturation is tangible. At KWV you can join a cellar tour in which the history of the co-op is explained, and taste a variety of premium wines and brandies. Tel 807 3007/8, open Mon-Fri 10am-3.45pm, weekends are for pre-booked groups only.

### Laborie
A supremely elegant manor house surrounded by lawns, oak trees, roses and vineyards, Laborie is the jewel of the Paarl wine route – and happens

to be in Paarl itself. Wine-tasting happens on a balcony with an enthralling view of the vineyards and the Drakenstein mountains. And Laborie's wines are generally exceptional, to boot. Tel 807 3390 (tastings), 807 3095 (restaurant), tastings Mon-Fri 9am-5pm (Sat in summer).

### Nederburg
A winelist without Nederburg is as rare as a virgin hooker. Nederburg has been making wine continuously for 200 years, and is probably the country's premier winemaker, with an exceptional record for dry whites. At the estate you can taste award-winning wines and admire the regal elegance of the classic Cape Dutch homestead. Cellar tours and light lunches are available by appointment. Tel 862 3104, open Mon-Fri 8.30am-5pm, Sat 8.30am-1pm, closed Sundays.

### Rhebokskloof
Rhebokskloof is one of very few estates open 365 days a year. The diminutive buck of its name can sometimes still be spotted on the picturesque slopes, which adjoin the Paarl Nature Reserve. For a formal wine-tasting which includes a talk, video screening and cellar tour, book with the estate a day in advance – but you can visit and taste anytime, any day. The Rhebokskloof restaurant (tel 863 8606) comes recommended. Tel 863 8386, open Mon-Sun 9am-5pm, including public holidays.

## •STELLENBOSCH ROUTE
Stellenbosch is home to students, wine, oak-trees, wine, academics, and wine. The town's stately tree-lined streets and many of its Cape Dutch houses date back to the 1680's. It's a peaceful but urbane place, and the undisputed heartbeat of the winelands, with the oldest and most diverse wine route (67 estates in total) in the Cape. If you don't have your own vehicle, you can get here easily by train from Cape Town station, and either join a wine tour or explore on foot or hire a bicycle. There's a convenient selection of restaurants in town, from continental to traditional Cape cuisine to pizza, and a wide range of overnight accommodation. The local Info office (tel 883 3544) and Wine Route hotline (tel 886 4310) are a good source of information. (See also page 34 for Day Trip info.)

### Alto
As the name implies, Alto is an upland estate, occupying the steep slopes of the dramatic Helderberg mountains. The farm's wine is of consistently good quality, with the cabernet sauvignon vintages winning global recognition. Alto's proprietor and winemaker is former Springbok rugby prop Hempies du Toit, who has decorated his homely tasting room with antique farm tools. Tel 881 3884, open Mon-Fri 9am-5pm, Sat 10am-4pm, closed Sun.

### Blaauwklippen
Blaauwklippen is a relaxed and friendly estate equipped for visitors, and home to a fascinating collection of vintage horse-carriages, vintage cars and antique furniture. You can take a ride in a horse-carriage and order a tasty "coachman's lunch" on the stoep. A wide range of wines are produced here, including the uncommon red variety, Zanfindel. A good choice if time is limited. Tel 880 0133, open Mon-Fri 9am-5pm, Sat 9am-1pm.

### Delaire
Delaire is a small winery of 44 hectares, beautifully perched on the crest of the Helshoogte mountain pass. At 300-500m above sea level the grapes ripen several weeks later than those of Stellenbosch below, resulting in excellent sauvignons, merlots, cabernets and chardonnays, all big in body

and soft on tannin. Enjoy a summer picnic under the oaks (tel 885 1756) or have a leisurely lunch at the Green Door Restaurant (tel 885 1149). E-mail delaire@iafrica.com, open Mon-Sat 10am-5pm, Sun 10-4pm.

## Jordan

Owned by the folks of Jordan Shoes fame, the kloof approach to this family-run farm is half the appeal. From the vantage point of the estate you can see Table Mountain, False Bay and the Stellenbosch valley. It's a remarkable view, and the farm's high-tech cellars and friendly vibe make it a pleasing stop. The wines are very good too – particularly the sauvignon blanc and chardonnay. Tel 881 3441, open Mon-Fri 10am-4.30pm, Sat 9.30am-2pm.

## Morgenhof

The French family who run Morgenhof, on the slopes of the stately Simonsberg, have ancestors who were making wine in the year 1210. The tradition continues with some choice Cape wines, especially the Morgenhof merlot. On sunny days, you can eat a sumptuous light lunch under the oaks, topped with fresh berries and ice cream, and in winter a hearty fireside luncheon is served in the gazebo. Tel 889 5510, open Mon-Fri 9am-5pm, Sat-Sun 10am-5pm (shorter hours in winter).

## Neethlingshof

Granted by Simon van der Stel to a one Willem Barend Lubbe in the 1600's, Neethlingshof is a well-established and glossy estate known for fine cabernet sauvignon, chardonnay and noble late harvest. The classic approach, through a long tunnel of towering pine trees that you'll recognise from the wine label, sets a perfect tone to laid-back quaffing and dining at either the Lord Neethling Restaurant or more relaxed and affordable Palm Terrace. Tel 883 8988, open Mon-Fri 9am-7pm, Sat-Sun 10am-4pm (summer).

## Overgaauw

Overgaauw was the first estate in South Africa to produce merlot and is known generally for excellent reds and ports. The architecture is Victorian – unusual for the Winelands – and the ambience low-key. Cellar tours take place by appointment on Wednesdays at 2.30pm; alternatively, consider making a full meal of Overgaauw by booking the wonderful self-catering cottage, an ex-shepherd's abode. Tel 881 3815, open Mon-Fri 8.30am-12.30pm, 2pm-5pm, Sat 10am-12.30pm, closed Sundays, R5 tasting fee.

## Rustenberg

At Rustenberg they don't make much fuss about visitors – it's a working farm with a low-key rural authenticity. The land has been under almost continuous wine cultivation since 1692, and two of the buildings are national monuments. On the wine front, the Rustenberg label is world-class, while the more affordable but very palatable Brampton label is also made here. No restaurant, but you are welcome to munch your own picnic under the oaks. Tel 809 1200, open Mon-Fri 9am-4.30pm, Sat 9am-12.30pm, no charge for tasting.

## Simonsig

Simonsig is renowned for Kaapse Vonkel, the first sparkling wine to be made using the Cap Classique method. The estate produces a dizzying range of top-quality wines, including an excellent ppinotage and chardonnay. No food is served, but you can enjoy a picnic at tables provided in the courtyard, and admire the valley below. Tel 888 4900, open Mon-Fri 10am-4.30pm, Sat 8.30am-4.30pm.

### Spier

The Spier Wine Estate is considerably more than just a wine farm – it's a veritable adult playpark. Among its attractions are vintage Cape Dutch architecture, a man-made lake surrounded by exquisite landscaped gardens, a superb outdoor amphitheatre that hosts local and international musical acts over the summer season, and a park for hand-reared cheetahs. Fine Cape cuisine can be savoured at the Jonkershuis Restaurant, while the farmstall compiles picnics for visitors. The 17th-century heritage of the estate is preserved in the Spier Manor House, where antiques, porcelain, and Dutch paintings are on display. And wine? Reds and whites bearing the Four Spears label are on sale, and they're pretty okay. Tel 809 1159, open Mon-Sun 9am-6pm (winter 9am-5pm).

### Want to know more?

There are a number of guides on the subject of fermented grapes but *John Platter's South African Wine Guide* (John and Erica Platter) leads the pack. Among South Africa's best-selling titles and updated annually, the book contains detailed reviews and ratings for virtually every local label. Indispensable reading for both the Tassenberg pleb and aspiring connoisseur. Available from most bookshops and wine stores.

## •world of birds

If it's got a beak, there's a fair chance you'll cross paths with it at the World of Birds, one of the largest bird parks on the planet. More than 330 species have their lodgings here, from bite-sized white-eyes to psychedelic macaws to Mad Max vultures and mystical owls. The park consists of over 100 walk-through aviaries: mammalian visitors are utterly ignored, passing incognito through a magical, fantastically diverse feathered universe. A captivating experience that would inspire even Alfred Hitchcock. Valley Rd, Hout Bay, tel 790 2730, open daily 9am-5pm.

# wot do you think?

gripes, praise, criticism, suggestions...

Let us have your view!

**Red Press**
**PO Box 23283**
**Claremont 7735**
**e-mail leger@mweb.co.za**

# a-z index

169 on Long 63
3rd i Gallery 9
89 on Roodebloem 68

## A

Abseil Africa 3, 29, 49
Action Paintball Games 102
Adult World 95
Adventure Village 3, 29, 49
Aero Sport 53
Africa Café 84
African Buzz Scooter Sales & Rentals 53
African Music Store 77
Africultural Tours 107
All Bar None 63
All Nations Club 64
Alphen Hotel 79
Alto 119
Angels 66
animal viewing 4
antique & junk shops 6
aquarium 6
Aquatrails 47
architecture 7
art galleries 9
Arts Association of Bellville 10
Ashbey's Galleries 13
Association for Visual Arts 10
Au Jardin 84
auctions 12

## B

Bacinis 85
ballooning 13
Bang the Gallery 10
Baraza 66, 83
Barnyard Farmstall 79
Barristers Grill & Café on Main 69, 85
bars 63
Baxter Theatre Centre 105
beaches 14, 25
Bead Sales 19
Bead Shop 19
bead shops 18
Beezy Bailey Art Factory 10
Beluga 85
Big Game Fishing Safaris 41
Bird-Watch Cape 21
birdwatching 19
Blaauwklippen 119
Black Marlin Restaurant 17
Blink 69
Bloemers Kosteater 85

Bloubergstrand 14
Blue Danube 85
Blue Mountain Adventures 92
Blues 83
Bo-Kaap 8, 23, 109
Bo-Kaap Guided Tour 8, 23
Bo-Kaap Museum 23, 57
boat cruises 21
bookshops 23
Boschendal 72, 117
Boulders 17, 19
Boye's Drive 18
braai spots 24
Brass Bell Restaurant 17, 79
Brendon Bell-Roberts Gallery 10
Bronx 66
Buena Vista Social Café 66
Buffelsbaai 16
Buitenverwachting 8, 72, 116
Bukhara 85
bungy jumping 25
Butterfly World 4

# C

cableway 26
Cabriere Estate 117
CAFDA 24
Café Adagio 79
Café Bardeli 86
Café Camissa 50
Café Dharma 86
Café Ganesh 69
Café Mozart 80
Café Paradiso 83
Café Sirens 69
Café Whatever 80
Caffé Balducci 85
Caledon Casino, Hotel & Spa 40
camel rides 27
Camel Rock Restaurant 16
Camps Bay 15
Canal Walk Shopping Centre 97
Cape Camel Rides 27
Cape Cobra Car Hire 30
Cape Colony 85
Cape Comedy Collective 31
Cape Gallery 10
Cape Gliding Club 41
Cape Medical Museum 57
Cape of Good Hope Nature Reserve 16, 19, 27, 61, 109
Cape Point 16, 33, 94
Cape Point Ostrich Farm 4
Cape Quad Trails 76
Cape Sport Centre 48, 115
Cape Sport Centre Kayak Rental 47
Cape Sugarbird Tours 21
Cape Town Concert Series 29

Cape Town Holocaust Centre 57
Cape Town Tourism Centre 9
Cape Tuna & Game Fishing Charters 41
Caprice 83
Carluccis 80
Castle of Good Hope 8, 28, 57
Cavendish Square 97
caving 28
Cellars-Hohenort 86
Chai Yo 86
Chamonix 117
Chapman's Peak 33, 94
Chilli 'n Lime 74
Church Street 6
Cinema Nouveau 56
Circe Launches 21
City Walk 109
Civair 43
Clara Anna Fontein Game Reserve 4
Classic Cape Charters 41
classic car hire 30
Classic Twin Tours 30, 54
classical music 29
Clifton 15
Club Galaxy 67
Club Georgia 64
Club Images 67
Club Unity 64
Club Vibe 67
clubs 63
CNA 24
Codfather 86
Coffee Lounge 64
Cohibar 64
comedy 30
Company Gardens 31
Company Gardens Restaurant 80
Computicket 29, 105
Constantia 116
Constantia Market 31
Constantia Nek 110
Cool Runnings 83
craft markets 31
cricket 99
Curve Bar 68
cycling 32

# D

Daily Deli 80
Darling 37
Day Trippers 49
day trips 34
De Goewerneur 86
Deer Park 54
Delaire 119
Den Anker Restaurant & Bar 67
Detour 66

Dias Tavern 86
Dieu Donné 117
District Six Museum 58
Diva 86
Dive Action 37
Dive Junction 38
diving 37
Dizzy Jazz Café 51
Dockside 68
Don Pedro's 68, 87
Doodles 84
Dorpstraat Café 74
Downhill Adventures 93, 102
Downhill Tours 55
Drum Café 39, 51
Drumbeat Charters 21
drumming 38
Dunes 84
Dusky Dive Academy 38

## E

Emily's Bistro 87
Everard Read Gallery 10
Evita se Perron 105, 108

## F

Fairview 118
Fairweather Yacht Charters 22
False Bay 114
Famous Butchers Grill 87
Far Side Adventures 38
Fedsure Park 99
Ferryman's Tavern 67
Fez 64
Fish Hoek 17
Fishmonger Hout Bay 87
Five Flies Restaurant & Bars 87
Floris Smit Huijs 87
fly-fishing 39
Foresters' Arms 69
Franschhoek 34, 116
Fujiyama 87

## G

Gallery Café 80
gambling 40
game fishing 40
Gardeners Cottage 82
Gauloises Warehouse 105
Getafix 64
Gignet Theatre Café 51
Gijima 64
Giovanni's Deliworld 80
gliding 41
go-karting 41
Golf Academy 42
golf-driving ranges 42
Gordon's Bay 18

Grand West Casino 40
Grange Theatre Café 106
Grassroute Tours 107
Green Dolphin 51
Green Point 110
Greenmarket Square 32, 43
Groot Constantia 8, 58, 80, 116
Groot Constantia Manor House 58
Groove Central 65
Guided City Walk 9

## H

Hänel Gallery 10
Happy Wok 87
Harbour Music Club 51
Harley-Davidson 54
Harvard Club 3
Hatfields 88
Haute Provence 117
Heaven 100
Helderberg Nature Reserve 62
helicopter flips 43
Hermanus 114
Hermanus Info 114
High Street Theatre 29, 106
hip-hop 50
Hofmeyr-Mills 13
Horse Racing 100
Horse Trail Safaris 44
horseriding 44
hot-air ballooning 13
Hout Bay 15, 45
Hout Bay Gallery 11
Hout Bay Market 32
Hout Bay Museum 45
Hustler Shop 95

## I

Ice Station 45
ice-skating 45
Imax 56
Imhoff Farm 11
Imhoff Farm Horse Rides 44
Imhoff Waldorf School 32
Independent Armchair Theatre 31, 51, 56
Indoor Grand Prix 42
Ingwe Africa Helicopter Charters 44

## J

J&B Met 100
Jagers Walk, Fish Hoek 110
jazz 50
Jet Lounge 65
jetskiing 46
Jo'burg 65
João Ferreira 11
Johans Borman Fine Art Gallery 11

Jonkershoek Nature Reserve 35
Jonkershoek Valley 55
Jordan 120
Josephine Mill 82
Josephine Mill Museum 58

## K

Kaapse Tafel 88
Kalk Bay 17
Kalk Bay Gallery 11
kayaking 46
Kenilworth Karting 42
Kennedy's Restaurant & Cigar Lounge 52
Kenny Finberg 13
Kilo shops 24
Kirstenbosch National Botanical Garden 72, 80, 88
Kirstenbosch Summer Concerts 29
Kite Shop 48
kite-flying 48
kite-surfing 48
Klein Constantia 8, 116
kloofing 49
Kommetjie 16, 20
Koopmans De Wet House 58
Kotobuki 88
Kronendal 8
Kuzma's 69
KWV 118

## L

L'Ormarins 118
La Colombe 88
La Med 66, 84
La Motte 117
La Playa 84
Labia 56
Laborie 118
Langebaan 37
Laser Quest 102
Le Bonheur Crocodile Farm 4
Le Cap 54
Le Petit Paris 81
Legend Tours 107
Lion's Head 111
Little Theatre 106
live music 49
Llandudno 15
Long Beach 17
Long Street Baths 103
Look & Listen 77

## M

Macassar 18
Maclear Beach 16
Maestros 88
Maharani 22
Maliblues 52

Mama Africa 52, 88
Mariner's Wharf 45
Marvol Museum of Russian Art & Culture 11
Mayibuye Archive 58
Maynardville Open-Air Theatre 106
Melissas 81
Melkbosstrand 14
Metrorail 108
Michaelis Collection 58
microlighting 53
Miller's Point 17
Milnerton 14
Mitaka Scooter Rentals 54
Monkey Town Primate Centre 5
Mont Rochelle 118
Montebello Design Centre 11
Monument Station 108
Moomba Club Sociale 65
More 65
Morgenhof 120
motorbike & scooter hire 53
Moulin Rouge Cabaret Bar 100
Mount Nelson Hotel 83
mountain biking 54
movies 56
Mr Pickwicks 88
Muizenberg 18
Muizenberg Pavilion 103
museums 57

# N

Naked on Kloof 88
Natale Labia Museum 59
nature reserves 61
Nedbank Imax Theatre 56
Nederburg 119
Neethlingshof 120
Nelson's Eye Restaurant & Grill 89
New York Bagels & Sitdown Deli 81
Newlands Forest 72, 111
Newlands Pool 103
Newlands Stadium 99
Newport Market & Deli 81
News Café 89
Nico Theatre Centre 106
nightlife 63
Noordhoek 15
Noordhoek Art Gallery 12
Noordhoek Beach Walk 111
Noordhoek Farm Village 32, 81
Nu-Metro 56
Nuisance Express 22

# O

Ocean Basket 89
Oceanrafters 22
Old Cape Bistro 81
Olympia Café & Deli 17, 81

On Broadway 52
On The Rocks 89
Oude Libertas Amphitheatre 106
Outlaw Records 77
Overgaauw 120

## P

Paarl 36, 118
Paarl Mountain Nature Reserve 36, 55
Paarl Tourism Bureau 36, 118
Paraglide Cape Town 70
paragliding 70
Parapente 71
Peanut Gallery 12
Peddlars on the Bend 81
Penguin Point Café 82
penguins 71
Peninsula Golf Driving Range 42
Piano Lounge 65
picnics 71
Pines Entertainment Centre 105
Pipe Track 111
Pizzeria Napoletana 89
Planetarium 73
Platboombaai 16
PNA 24
poetry readings 73
pool bars 74
Pre-perused books 24
Primi Piatti 82
Purple Turtle 52
putt-putt 75
Putt-Putt Enterprise 75

## Q

quad biking 76
Quay 4 Restaurant & Tavern 67

## R

Radisson Hotel 83
Ratanga Junction 76
Real Cape Adventures 47
record & CD shops 77
Red Herring 70, 82
Rembrandt van Rijn Art Gallery 12
Rent 'n Ride 46, 55, 93
restaurants 78
Rheboksloof 119
Rhodes House 65
Rhodes Memorial 90
Rhodes Memorial Restaurant 82
Rhythm Divine 66
Ride 'n Dine 26
Rietvlei Nature Reserve 20
River Club 42, 75
Robben Island 91
Robertsvallei 34
rock-climbing 92

roller-blading 92
Rondevlei Nature Reserve 5, 20, 62
Rose Korber Art Consultancy 12
Ruby In The Dust 52
rugby 99
Rugby Museum 59
Rugged Viny 77
Rust-en-Vreugd 59
Rustenberg 120

## S

SA Astronomical Observatory 73
SA National Gallery 98
SA Naval Museum 60
SA Windsurfaris & Rentals 115
Saldanha 37
SANCOB 20
Sandbar 84
sandboarding 93
Sandy Bay 15
Scarborough 16
scenic drives 93
scratch patches 94
Sea Point 15
Sea Point Pavilion 103
Sea Point Promenade 111
Sessions Music World 78
sex shops 95
shark diving 95
shopping malls 96
Signal Hill 94, 97
Silvermine Nature Reserve 20, 25, 61, 72, 112
Silvermine South 55
Silvertree Restaurant 88
Simon's Town 112
Simon's Town Museum 60
Simonsig 120
Skydive Citrusdal 98
skydiving 97
Sleepy Hollow Horse Riding 44
Snake Centre 5
snorkelling 38
soccer 99
South African Cultural History Museum 60
South African Jewish Museum 59
South African Maritime Museum 59
South African Museum 60
South African National Gallery 12
South Coast Seafaris 96
spectator sport 99
Speleological Association 29
Spier Cheetah Park 5
Spier Summer Festival 29
Spier Vintage Train 108
Spier Wine Estate 72, 106, 121
Sport Helicopters 44
Springfield 2 69

St James 18
Steamboat Vicky 22
Steenberg Vineyards 116
Stellenbosch 35, 119
Ster-Kinekor 56
Ster-Kinekor Cinema Nouveau 56
Stones (Cape Town) 74
Stones (Observatory) 74
Strand 18
Strandfontein 18
strip clubs 100
sundowners 83
surfing 100
survival games 102
Sweet Sunshine 22
swimming pools 102
Syndicate Records 78

# T

Table Bay Diving 38
Table Mountain 26, 103, 112
Table Mountain Bistro 84
Taboo 69
Tafelberg Road 94, 112
Tana-Baru Cultural Tours 107
Telkom Exploratorium 60
ten-pin bowling 104
The Jam 51, 65
The Lounge 65
The Restaurant 89
The Shack 75
theatre 105
Theatre On The Bay 107
Thunder Bikes 54
Ticketline 56
Tigger Too Charter Exclusive Cruises 22
Tokai Forest 25, 54, 73, 112
Tokai Manor House 8
Township Music Tours 108
township tours 107
train trips 108
Two Oceans Aquarium 6, 62
Two Oceans Restaurant 27
Tyger Valley Centre 97
Tygerberg Nature Reserve 62
Tygerberg Zoo 5

# U

UCT Irma Stern Museum 12
Ultimate Angling 39
University of Stellenbosch Art Gallery 12

# V

V&A Waterfront 113
Velddrif 37
Venture Forth Rock Climbing 92
Victoria Wharf Shopping Centre 97
Vilamoura 89

Village Café 82
Vineyard Hotel 83

## W

walks 109
Warrior Toy Museum 60
Waterfront 113
Waterfront Adventures 23
Waterfront Charters 23
Waterfront Craft Market 32
West Coast 36, 114
West Coast National Park 37
West End 52
Western Cape Action Tours 108
Western Province Racing Club 100
Wetbikes Cape Town 46
whale-watching 113
Wharfside Grill 90
White Shark Ecoventures 96
White Shark Projects 96
Wiesenhof 5
Wild Fig 90
wildlife 4
William Fehr Collection 28
Willoughby & Co 90
windsurfing 114
wine routes 115
Wine Valley Horse Trails 44
Winelands Ballooning 13
World of Birds 6, 20, 45, 121

## Y

Yellow Submarine 46
Yzerfontein 36

## Z

Zero932 90
zoos 4

# notes

## notes

## notes

## notes

# notes